Patterns and Parkas

Investigating Geometric Principles, Shapes, Patterns, and Measurement

Part of the Series

Math in a Cultural Context:

Lessons Learned from Yup'ik Eskimo Elders

Grade 2

Sandi Pendergrast

Jerry Lipka

Daniel Lynn Watt

Kay Gilliland

Nancy Sharp

Developed by the University of Alaska Fairbanks, Fairbanks, Alaska

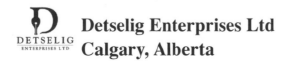

Detselig Enterprises Ltd
Calgary, Alberta

Math in a Cultural Context: Lessons Learned from Yup'ik Eskimo Elders© was developed at the University of Alaska Fairbanks. This material is based upon work supported by the U.S. Department of Education grant #S356A030033, Developing and Implementing Culturally Based Curriculum and Teacher Preparation, and the National Science Foundation under grant #9618099, Adapting Yup'ik Elders' Knowledge: Pre-K-to-6th Math and Instructional Materials Development.

 This project was also sponsored, in part, by the University of Alaska Fairbanks and the Bristol Bay Curriculum Project.

Library and Archives Canada Cataloguing in Publication

Patterns and parkas : investigating geometric principles, shapes, patterns and measurement / Sandi
    Pendergrast ... [et al.].

(Math in a cultural context: lessons learned from Yup'ik Eskimo elders)
ISBN-13: 978-1-55059-325-9
ISBN-10: 1-55059-325-0

1. Mathematics—Study and teaching (Primary) 2. Yupik Eskimos—Alaska.
I. Pendergrast, Sandi II. Series.

QA135.6.P38 2006   372.7'044

C2006-904225-X

Detselig Enterprises Ltd. acknowledges the financial support of the Government of Canada through the Book Publishing Industry Development Program (BPIDP) for our publishing activities. We also acknowledge the support of the Alberta Foundation for the Arts for our publishing program.
Detselig Enterprises Ltd.
210-1220 Kensington Rd. NW, Calgary, AB, T2N 3P5 Canada
Phone: (403) 283-0900/Fax: (403) 283-6947/E-mail: temeron@telusplanet.net
www.temerondetselig.com
ISBN: 1-55059-325-0
SAN: 113-0234
Printed in Canada

MATH IN A CULTURAL CONTEXT©

MCC

*Principal Investigator, Writer,
and Series Editor:*
Jerry Lipka

Project Mathematician:
Barbara L. Adams

Project Manager:
Flor Banks

Literacy:
Joan Parker Webster

Project Illustrator:
Putt (Elizabeth) Clark

Project Layout:
Mary Haley
Sue Mitchell
Beverly Peterson

Editing:
Carrie Aldrich
Mary Haley
Sue Mitchell
Jill Osier

Folklorist:
Ben Orr

Math Consultant:
Anthony Rickard

CD-ROM and DVD Creators:
Ben and Eliza Orr
Maya Salganek

Teachers Piloting the Module:
Rebecca Adams
Barbara Arena
Katherine M. Brown
Kathie Chilcott
Ann Edwards
Deborah Endicott
Don Everhart
Gretchen Frank
Mary George
Lois Marie Heine
Frank Hendrickson
Ann Johnson
Sophie Kasayulie
Janann Kaufman
Annie Kinegak
Elizabeth Lake
Eileen Levison
Anecia Lomack
Elizabeth Merideth
Melissa Moede
Judy Morotti
Gretchen Murphy
Sharlee L. Reabold
Nancy Sharp
Beth Smith
Christine Villano

Yup'ik Elders:
Mary Active
Henry Alakayak
Mary Bavilla
Winifred Beans
Annie Blue
Lillie Gamechuk Pauk
Theresa Mike
Anuska Nanalook

Yup'ik Consultants:
Dora Andrew-Ihrke
Mary Beans
Walkie Charles
Grace Gamechuk
Mary George
Marie Napoka
Eliza Orr
Sassa Peterson
Ferdinand Sharp
Anecia Toyukak
Nastasia Wahlberg
Evelyn Yanez

Table of Contents

Acknowledgements

From Jerry Lipka, Series Editor

It is now almost twenty-five years since I started working with Dora Andrew-Ihrke, Nancy and Ferdinand Sharp, and Evelyn Yanez, and to this day I continue to find myself learning from them. What a pleasure! This module, *Patterns and Parkas,* came to fruition because of their willingness to share their cultural knowledge, and their ability to make connections between Yup'ik knowledge and school-based math. Over the many years of working together, a way of teaching has emerged which shifts the role of the teacher and changes the classroom atmosphere and norms. Expert-apprentice modeling, joint productive activity, and cognitive apprenticeship are some of the teaching practices that have emerged through their classroom teaching and analysis. These practices were once considered "too Yup'ik" to be part of schooling; now they permeate this module and others in this series. For their contributions to this project and to the field of education, this module is dedicated to Dora Andrew-Ihrke, Nancy Sharp, Ferdinand Sharp and Evelyn Yanez. Thank you.

Thanks also to elders Winifred Beans and Theresa Mike of St. Marys, and Mary Active, Mary Bavilla, and Annie Blue of Togiak, Alaska, all of whom have shared their knowledge of telling stories and making patterns. Elias Polty and Lilly Afcan have contributed their cultural knowledge, creativity, and ingenuity in developing songs and dances that extend the scope of this module. We would like to further acknowledge the contributions of Frederick George and Sam Ivan of Akiachak and Akiak, Alaska, who have supported and joined us in our efforts to produce this particular module as well as all of the modules in this series.

The supplemental math series *Math in a Cultural Context: Lessons Learned from Yup'ik Eskimo Elders* is based on traditional and present-day wisdom and is dedicated to the late Mary George of Akiachak, her late father George Moses of Akiachak, and to the late Lillie Gamechuk Pauk of Manokotak, Alaska. Mary contributed to every aspect of this long-term project, with her unique ideas, her warm acceptance of people from all walks of life, and her ways of connecting traditional Yup'ik knowledge with modern Western knowledge. Without the dedication and perseverance of Mary and her husband, Frederick George, who tirelessly continues to work with this project, this work would not be possible. Mary George and Marie Napoka, of Tuluksak, Alaska, first collected the pattern designs that elders shared with them, and those pattern pieces are the foundation of this module.

George Moses was always eager and willing to teach and share his knowledge of the land and river. He was particularly concerned with the well-being of the next generation and hoped that this project would help connect community knowledge to schooling. Lillie Gamechuk Pauk cheerfully worked with this project even when she was ill. She would make sure that she first told her story to the group before she attended to other personal concerns. Her dedication, laughter, and spirit of giving formed a foundation for this project. For more years than we care to remember, I have had the pleasure to work with and learn from Ferdinand Sharp and Sassa Peterson of Manokotak, Alaska. Their contributions are immeasurable, as is their friendship. Our long-term relationship with elders who embraced this work wholeheartedly has made this difficult endeavor pleasurable as we learn from each other. In particular, I would like to acknowledge Henry Alakayak of Manokotak and Annie Blue of Togiak, whose dedication and commitment to cultural continuity has greatly inspired our project. They have set examples of perseverance toward creating culturally relevant school curricula. Mary Active and Mary E.

Bavilla from Togiak and Anuska Nanalook from Manokotak also contributed unselfishly. They came with stories that enriched us. Anecia and Mike Toyukak of Manokotak shared their knowledge about many aspects of traditional life—from Anecia's gifted storytelling and storyknifing, to how kayaks and other traditional Yup'ik crafts were made, to countless stories on how to survive. All of this valuable information contributed to this and other modules.

We would like to thank our dedicated staff, especially Flor Banks, who has spent countless hours editing and ensuring that this project was completed. Her highly refined organization skills, determination to get the job done, and motivation to move this project forward are some of the ways that she has contributed to this project. She has been a pleasure to work with, and she has done it all with a smile. To Putt Clark, graphic artist extraordinaire, who kept up with every demand and produced more and better artwork than anyone could have hoped for and who has worked with this project from its inception—thank you. To Barbara Adams, who has done an outstanding job as project mathematician and so much more. Her clear-headed thinking and mathematical insights contributed so much depth to these modules, and we appreciate her perseverance and dedication to seeing this project through. Thank you. To Dan Watt, whose proofing, editing, and math suggestions improved this module. To Eliza and Ben Orr for all their hard work and for producing the Yup'ik Glossary, an outstanding piece of work that continues to evolve and that accompanies this project. We thank Maya Salganek who produced the DVD *Tumartat: Putting the Pieces Together to Make a Whole,* which is a wonderful piece of work and like the Orr's contribution extends this module and this series in some new and important directions. To Mary Haley and Sue Mitchell for their editing and layout work, which has ensured that these modules are user-friendly and accessible. To Joan Parker-Webster for her literacy and pedagogical insights. Thank you, Joan. Anthony Rickard has brought a wealth of experience in reform-oriented math. Being no stranger to Alaska, he has made insightful connections between math and the Alaska context. By adding math problems and providing tight readings of the text, his work has strengthened this product. Also thanks to Wendy Wood, Kellie Oxie, Kristy Nicholas, Jessica Potrikus, Linda Sheldon, and Alice Atuk for their continued support behind the scenes, which enables products like to this to come to fruition.

A special thanks to the Anchorage School District, the Fairbanks North Star Borough School District, the Lower Yukon School District, the Yupiit School District, the St. Marys School District, the Yukon Flats School District, the Nenana City School District, and to the Southwest Region Schools for their cooperation in piloting modules. And thanks to all other math writers, project and pilot teachers, and elders who have helped with this project.

This has been a long-term and collaborative endeavor, and I hope that we have met the expectations of so many elders who shared their knowledge so freely. Last but not least, to my loving wife, Janet Schichnes, who supported me in countless ways that allowed me to complete this work, and to my children, Alan and Leah.

Introduction

Math in a Cultural Context: Lessons Learned from Yup'ik Eskimo Elders

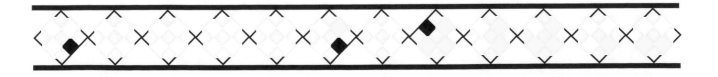

Introduction to the Series

Math in a Cultural Context: Lessons Learned from Yup'ik Eskimo Elders (MCC) is a supplemental math curriculum based on the traditional wisdom and practices of the Yup'ik Eskimo people of southwest Alaska. The kindergarten-to-seventh-grade math modules you are about to teach are the result of almost two decades of collaboration among math educators, teachers, and Yup'ik Eskimo elders to connect cultural knowledge to school mathematics. To understand the rich environment from which this curriculum came, imagine traveling on a snowmachine over the frozen tundra and finding your way based on the position of the stars in the night sky. Consider paddling a sleek kayak across open waters shrouded in fog, yet knowing by the pattern of the waves which way to travel toward land. Or imagine building a kayak or making clothing and accurately sizing them by visualizing or using body measures. This is a small sample of the activities that modern Yup'ik people engage in. The mathematics embedded in these activities formed the basis for this series of supplemental math modules. Each module is independent and lasts from three to eight weeks.

From 2001 through spring 2006, with the exception of one urban trial, students who used these modules consistently outperformed at statistically significant levels over students who only used their regular math textbooks. This was true for urban as well as rural students, both Caucasian and Alaska Native. We believe that this supplemental curriculum will motivate your students and strengthen their mathematical understanding because of the engaging content, the hands-on approach to problem solving, and the emphasis on mathematical communication. Further, these modules build on students' everyday experience and intuitive understandings, particularly in geometry, a subject that is under-represented in schools.

A design principle used in the development of these modules is that the activities allow students to explore mathematical concepts semiautonomously. Through the use of hands-on materials, students can "physically" prove conjectures, solve problems, generalize, and find patterns, properties, and shortcuts. The activities incorporate multiple modalities and can challenge students with diverse intellectual needs. Hence, the curriculum is designed for heterogeneous groups, with the realization that different students will tap into different cognitive strengths. According to Sternberg and his colleagues (1997, 1998), by engaging students creatively, analytically, and practically, students will have a more robust understanding of the concept. This allows for shifting roles and expertise among students rather than privileging those students with analytic knowledge.

The modules explore the everyday application of mathematical skills such as grouping, approximating, measuring, proportional thinking, informal geometry, and counting in base twenty, and then the modules present these in terms of formal mathematics. Students move from the concrete and applied to more formal and abstract math. The activities are designed for students to:
*   learn to solve mathematical problems that support an in-depth understanding of mathematical concepts;
*   derive mathematical formulas and rules from concrete and practical applications;
*   become flexible thinkers by learning that there is more than one method of solving a mathematical problem;
*   learn to communicate and think mathematically while they demonstrate understanding to peers; and
*   learn content across the curriculum, since the lessons comprise Yup'ik Eskimo culture, literacy, geography, and science.

Beyond meeting some of the content (mathematics) and process standards of the National Council of Teachers of Mathematics (2000), the curriculum design and its activities respond to the needs of diverse learners. Many activities are designed for group work. One of the strategies for using group work is to provide leadership opportunities to students who may not typically be placed in that role. Also, the modules tap into a wide array of intellectual abilities—practical, creative, and analytic. We assessed modules tested in rural and urban Alaska and found that students who were only peripherally involved in math became more active participants when using this curriculum.

Our goal is for students to learn to reason mathematically by constructing models and analyzing practical tasks for their embedded mathematics. This enables them to generate and discover mathematical rules and formulas. In this way, we offer students a variety of ways to engage the math material through practical activity, spatial/visual learning, analytic thinking, and creative thinking. Students are constantly encouraged to communicate mathematically by presenting their understandings while other students are encouraged to provide alternate solutions, strategies, and counter arguments. This process also strengthens their deductive reasoning.

Pedagogical Approaches Used in the Modules

The concept of third space is embedded within each module. Third space relates to a dynamic and creative place between school-based knowledge, everyday knowledge, and knowledge related to other nonmainstream cultural groups. Third space also includes local knowledge such as ways of measuring and counting that are distinct from school-based notions, and it is about bringing these elements together in a creative, respectful, and artful manner. Within this creative and evolving space, pedagogical content knowledge can develop creatively from both Western schooling and local ways. In particular, this module pays close attention to expert-apprentice modeling because of its prevalent use among Yup'ik elders and other Alaska Native groups.

Design

The curriculum design includes strategies that engage students

- cognitively, so that students use a variety of thinking strategies (analytic, creative, and practical);
- socially, so that students with different social, cognitive, and mathematical skills can use those strengths to lead and help solve mathematical problems;
- pedagogically, so that students explore mathematical concepts and communicate and learn to reason mathematically by demonstrating their understanding of the concepts; and
- practically, as students apply or investigate mathematics to solve problems from their daily lives.

The organization of the modules follows five distinct approaches to teaching and learning that converge into one system.

Expert-Apprentice Modeling

The first approach, expert-apprentice modeling, comes from Yup'ik elders and teachers and is supported by research in anthropology and education. Many lessons begin with the teacher (the expert) demonstrating a concept to the students (the apprentices). Following the theoretical position of the Russian psychologist Vygotsky (cited in Moll, 1990) and expert Yup'ik teachers and elders (Lipka and Yanez, 1998), students begin to appropriate the knowledge of the teacher (who functions in the role of expert), as the teacher and the more adept apprentices help other students learn. This establishes a collaborative classroom setting in which student-to-student and student-to-teacher dialogues are part of the classroom fabric.

More recently, we have observed experienced teachers using joint productive activity, where the teacher works in parallel with students modeling an activity, a concept, or a skill. When effectively implemented, joint productive activity appears to increase student ownership of the task and increases their responsibility and motivation. The typical authority structure surrounding classrooms changes as students take on more of the responsibility for learning. Social relations in the classroom become more level. In the case of this module the connections between out-of-school learning and in-school learning are strengthened through pedagogical approaches such as expert-apprentice modeling and joint productive activity when those are approaches of the community.

Reform-oriented Approach

The second pedagogical approach emphasizes student collaboration in solving "deeper" problems (Ma, 1999). This approach is supported by research in math classrooms and particularly by recent international studies (Stevenson et al., 1990; Stigler and Hiebert, 1998) strongly suggesting that math problems should be more in-depth and challenging and that students should understand the underlying principles, not merely use procedures competently. The modules present complex problems (two-step, open-ended problems) that require students to think more deeply about mathematics.

Multiple Intelligences

These modules tap into students' multiple intelligences. While some students may learn best from hands-on problems related to the real world, others may learn best when abstracting and deducing. This module provides opportunities to guide both modalities. Robert Sternberg's work (1997, 1998) influenced the development of these modules. He has consistently found that students who are taught so that they use their analytic, creative, and practical intelligences will outperform students who are taught using one modality, most often analytic. Thus, we have shaped our activities to engage students on all three levels.

Mathematical Argumentation and Deriving Rules

The purpose of math communication, argumentation, and conceptual understanding is to foster students' mathematical reasoning. These modules support a math classroom environment in which students explore the underlying mathematical rules as they solve problems. Through structured classroom communication, students will learn to work collaboratively in a problem solving environment in which they learn to both appreciate and evaluate alternative solutions strategies and solutions. They will present their mathematical solutions to their peers and, when faced with discrepancies, will communicate their strategies, helping others understand their reasoning and mathematical decisions. Mathematical discussions are encouraged in order to strengthen students' mathematical and logical thinking as they share their findings. This requires classroom norms that support student communication and learning from errors rather than criticizing them. Activities in the module are organized by connecting tasks and materials so that the possible explorations are limited, increasing the likelihood that students will understand the concept or deduce principles. Students are given the opportunity to support their conceptual understanding by practicing it in the context of a particular problem.

Familiar and Unfamiliar Contexts Challenge Students' Thinking

By working in unfamiliar settings and facing new and challenging problems, students learn to think creatively. They gain confidence in their abilities to solve both everyday problems and abstract mathematical questions, and their entire realm of knowledge and experience expands. Further, by making the familiar unfamiliar and by working on novel problems, students are encouraged to connect what they learn from one setting (everyday problems) with mathematics in another setting. For example, most sixth-grade students know about rectangles and how to calculate the area of a rectangle, but if you ask students to go outside and find the four corners of an eight-foot-by-twelve-foot-rectangle without using rulers or similar instruments, they are faced with a challenging problem. As they work through this everyday application (which is needed to build any rectangular structure) and as they "prove" to their classmates that they do, in fact, have a rectangular base, they expand their knowledge of rectangles. In effect, they must shift their thinking from considering rectangles as physical entities or prototypical examples to understanding the salient properties of a rectangle. Similarly, everyday language, conceptions, and intuition may, in fact, be in the way of mathematical understanding and the precise meanings of mathematical terms. By treating familiar knowledge in unfamiliar ways, students explore and confront their own mathematical understandings and begin to understand the world of mathematics. This concept guides the overall pedagogical approach to the modules.

The Organization of the Modules

The curriculum includes modules for kindergarten through seventh grade. Modules are divided into sections—activities, explorations, and exercises—with some variation between modules. Supplementary information is included in Cultural Notes, Teacher Notes, and Math Notes. Each module follows a particular cultural story line, to which the mathematics are directly connected. Some modules are designed around a children's story, and an illustrated text is included for the teacher to read to the class.

The module is a teacher's manual. It begins with a general overview of the activities ahead, an explanation of the math and pedagogy of the module, teaching suggestions, and a historical and cultural overview of the specific module and the curriculum in general. Each activity includes an introductory statement, an estimated duration, goals, materials, any preclass preparatory instructions for the teacher, and the procedures for the class follow. Assessments are placed both throughout and at the end of activities.

Illustrations help to enliven the text. Yup'ik stories and games are interspersed and enrich the mathematics. Transparency masters, worksheet masters, and suggestions for additional materials are attached at the end of each activity. An overhead projector is necessary. Blackline masters that can be made into overhead transparencies are an important visual enhancement of the activities, stories, and games. Such visual aids also help in furthering classroom discussion and understanding.

Resources and Materials Required to Teach the Modules

Materials

Each module and each activity lists all of the materials and learning tools necessary to carry it out. Some of the tools are expressly mathematical, such as interlocking centimeter cubes, abaci, and compasses. Others are particular to the given context of the problem, such as latex and black-and-white geometric pattern pieces. Many of the materials are items a teacher will probably have on hand, such as paper, markers, scissors, and rulers. Students learn how to manipulate the materials and, in the process, gain important mathematical and cultural knowledge. The value of caring for the materials is underscored by the precepts of subsistence, which is based on processing raw materials and foods with maximum use and minimum waste. Periodically, food is used in an activity; in such instances, we encourage minimal waste.

For materials and learning tools that are more difficult to find or that are directly related to unique aspects of this curriculum, we provide detailed instructions for the teacher and students on how to make those tools. For example, in *Going to Egg Island: Adventures in Grouping and Place Values,* students use a base twenty abacus. Although the project has produced and makes available a few varieties of wooden abaci, detailed instructions are provided for the teacher and students on how to make simple, inexpensive, and usable abaci with beads and pipe cleaners.

The materials and tools limit the range of mathematical possibilities, guiding students' explorations so that they focus upon the intended purpose of the lesson. For example, in one module, latex sheets are used to explore concepts of topology. Students can manipulate the latex to the degree necessary to discover the mathematics of the various activities and apply the rules of topology.

DVDs

To more vividly convey the knowledge of the elders underlying the entire curriculum, we have produced a few DVDs to accompany some of the modules. For example, the module *Going to Egg Island: Adventures in Grouping and Place Values* includes DVDs of Yup'ik elders demonstrating some traditional Yup'ik games. We also include footage and recordings of the ancient chants that accompanied these games. This module includes the DVD *Tumartat: Putting the Pieces Together to Make a Whole.*

Yup'ik Language Glossary and Math Terms Glossary

To help teachers and students get a better feel for the Yup'ik language, its sounds, and the Yup'ik words used to describe mathematical concepts in this curriculum, we have developed a Yup'ik glossary on CD-ROM. Each word is recorded in digital form and can be played back in Yup'ik. The context of the word is provided, giving teachers and students a better sense of the Yup'ik concept, not just its Western "equivalent." Pictures and illustrations often accompany the word for additional clarification.

Yup'ik Values

There are many important Yup'ik values associated with each module. The elders value listening, learning, working hard, being cooperative, passing knowledge on to others, and not being wasteful. These values are expressed in the Yup'ik stories that accompany the modules as well as in the cultural notes and in various activities. Yup'ik people continue to make and build crafts from raw materials. Since these modules are fashioned around such themes as making Yup'ik border patterns and building model kayaks, and since this aspect of the culture is reflected in the modules, students who engage in these modules will learn how to make simple mathematical tools fashioned around such themes as Yup'ik border patterns and building model kayaks, fish racks, and smokehouses.

Cultural Notes

Most of the mathematics used in the curriculum comes from our direct association and long-term collaboration with Yup'ik Eskimo elders and teachers. Each module is based on a cultural activity and follows a Yup'ik cultural story line along which the activities and lessons unfold. We have included many cultural notes to describe and explain more fully the origins, purposes, and variations associated with a particular traditional activity.

Math Notes

We want to ensure that teachers who may want to teach these modules but feel unsure of some of the mathematical concepts will feel supported by the Math Notes. These provide background material to help teachers better understand the mathematical concepts presented in the activities and exercises of each module. For example, in the *Perimeter and Area* module, the Math Notes give a detailed description of a rectangle and describe the geometric proofs one would apply to ascertain whether or not a shape is a rectangle. One module explores rectangular prisms and the geometry of three-dimensional objects; the Math Notes include information on the geometry of rectangular prisms, including proofs, to facilitate the instructional process. In every module, connections are made between the "formal math," its practical application, and the classroom strategies for teaching the math.

Teacher Notes

The main function of the Teacher Notes is to focus on the key pedagogical aspects of the lesson. For example, they provide suggestions on how to facilitate students' mathematical understanding through classroom organization strategies, classroom communication, and ways of structuring lessons. Teacher Notes also make suggestions for ways of connecting out-of-school knowledge with schooling.

Assessment

Assessment and instruction are interrelated throughout the modules. Assessments are embedded within instructional activities, and teachers are encouraged to carefully observe, listen, and challenge their students' thinking. We call this active assessment, which allows teachers to assess how well students have learned to solve the mathematical and cultural problems introduced in each module.

Careful attention has been given to developing assessment techniques and tools that evaluate both the conceptual and procedural knowledge of students. We agree with Ma (1999) that having one type of knowledge without the other, or not understanding the link between the two, will produce only partial understanding. The goal here is to produce relational understanding in mathematics. Instruction and assessment have been developed and aligned to ensure that both types of knowledge are acquired; this has been accomplished using both traditional and alternative techniques. The specific details and techniques for assessment (when applicable) are included within activities. The three main tools for collecting and using assessment data follow.

Math Notebooks

In recent years, NCTM has promoted standards that incorporate math notebooks as part of math instruction. Journaling has often occurred as a tool for students to reflect on what was learned. In contrast, math notebooks are used by students to record what they are thinking and learning about math concepts before, during, and after the activities in the modules. Through the use of math notebooks, students build their content knowledge while developing their literacy skills through reading, writing, drawing, and graphic representations. Math notebooks also play an important role in helping students develop math vocabulary.

Observation

Observing and listening to students lets teachers learn about the strategies they use to analyze and solve various problems. Listening to informal conversations between students as they work cooperatively on problems provides further insight into their strategies. Through observation, teachers also learn about their students' attitudes toward mathematics and their skills in cooperating with others. Observation is an excellent way to link assessment with instruction.

Adaptive Instruction

The goal of the summary assessment in this curriculum is to adapt instruction to the skills and knowledge needed by a group of students. From reviewing notebook notes to simply observing students, teachers learn which mathematical processes their students are able to effectively use and which ones they need to practice more. Adaptive assessment and instruction complete the link between assessment and instruction.

An Introduction to the Land and Its People, Geography, and Climate

Flying over the largely uninhabited expanse of southwest Alaska on a dark winter morning, one looks down at a white landscape interspersed with trees, winding rivers, rolling hills, and mountains. One sees a handful of lights sprinkled here and there. Half of Alaska's 600,000-plus population lives in Anchorage; the other half is dispersed among smaller cities such as Fairbanks and Juneau and among the over 200 rural villages that are scattered across the state. After landing on a village airstrip, which is usually gravel and, in winter, covered with smooth, hard-packed snow, one is taken to the village by either car or snowmachine. Few villages or regional centers are connected to a road system, so transportation between these communities is by small plane, boat, or snowmachine, depending on the season.

It is common for the school to be centrally located. Village roads are usually unpaved, and people drive cars, four-wheelers, and snowmachines. Houses are typically made from modern materials and have electricity and running water. Over the past 20 years, Alaska villages have undergone major changes, both technologically and culturally. Most now have television, a full phone system, modern water and sewage treatment facilities, an airport, and a small store. Some also have a restaurant, and a few even have a small hotel and taxicab service. Access to medical care is still sporadic, usually provided by a local health care worker and a community health clinic, or by health care workers from larger cities or regional centers who visit on a regular basis. Serious medical emergencies require air evacuation to either Anchorage or Fairbanks.

The Schools

Years of work have gone into making education as accessible as possible to rural communities. Almost every village has an elementary school, and most have a high school. Some also have a higher education satellite facility, computer access to higher education courses, or options that enable students to earn college credits while in their respective home communities. Vocational education is taught in some of the high schools, and there are also special vocational education facilities in some villages. While English has become the dominant language throughout Alaska, many Yup'ik children in the villages still learn Yup'ik at home.

Yup'ik Village Life Today

Although many modern conveniences are located within the village, when one steps outside of its narrow bounds, one is immediately aware of one's vulnerability in this immense and unforgiving land, where one misstep can lead to disaster. Knowledgeable elders know how to cross rivers and find their way through ice fields, navigating the seemingly featureless tundra by using directional indicators such as frozen grass and the constellations in the night sky. All of this can mean the difference between life and death. In the summer, when this largely treeless, moss- and grass-covered plain thaws into a large swamp dotted with small lakes, the consequences of ignorance, carelessness, and inexperience can be just as devastating. Underwater hazards in the river, such as submerged logs, can capsize a boat, dumping the occupants into the cold, swift current. Overland travel is much more difficult during the warm months due to the marshy ground and many waterways, and one can easily become disoriented and get lost. The sea is also integral to life in this region and requires its own set of skills and specialized knowledge to be safely navigated.

The Importance of the Land: Hunting and Gathering

Most villagers continue to participate in the seasonal rounds of hunting, fishing, and gathering. Depending upon their location (coastal community, riverine, or interior), villagers hunt and gather the surrounding resources. These include sea mammals, fish, caribou, and many types of berries. The seasonal subsistence calendar illustrates which activities take place during the year (see Figure i). Basic subsistence skills include knowing how to read the sky to determine the weather and make appropriate travel plans, being able to read the land to find one's way, knowing how to build an emergency shelter, and, in the greater scheme, knowing how to hunt and gather food and properly process and store it. In addition, the byproducts of subsistence activities, such as walrus tusks, pelts, and skins, are then made into clothing, decorative items, and a variety of other utilitarian arts and crafts products. They provide an important source of cash for many rural residents.

Hunting and gathering are still of great importance in modern Yup'ik society. A young man's first seal hunt is celebrated. Family members who normally live and work in one of the larger cities will often fly home to help when the salmon are running. Whole families still gather to go berry picking. The importance of hunting and gathering in daily life is further reflected in the legislative priorities expressed by rural residents in Alaska. These focus on such things as subsistence hunting regulations, fishing quotas, resource development, and environmental issues that affect the well-being of subsistence resources.

Conclusion

We developed this curriculum in a Yup'ik context with good results with Yup'ik and non-Yup'ik students.. The traditional subsistence and other skills of the Yup'ik people incorporate spatial, geometrical, and proportional reasoning and other mathematical reasoning. We have attempted to offer you and your students a new way to approach and apply mathematics while also learning about Yup'ik culture. Our goal has been to present math as practical information that is inherent in everything we do. We hope your students will adopt and incorporate some of this knowledge and add it to their learning base.

The elders who guided this work emphasized that the next generation of children should be flexible thinkers and leaders. In a small way, we hope that this curriculum guides you and your students along this path.

Tua-i-ngunrituq [This is not the end].

References

Lipka, Jerry, and Evelyn Yanez. 1998. Identifying and understanding cultural differences: Toward culturally based pedagogy. In Transforming the culture of schools: Yup'ik Eskimo examples. Mahwah, NJ: Lawrence Erlbaum and Associates.

Ma, Liping. 1999. Knowing and teaching elementary mathematics. Mahwah, NJ: Lawrence Erlbaum.

Moll, Luis. 1990. Vygotksy and education: Instructional implications and applications of sociohistorical psychology. Cambridge: Cambridge University Press.

National Council of Teachers of Mathematics. 2000. Principles and standards for school mathematics. Reston, VA: National Council of Teachers of Mathematics.

Sternberg, Robert. 1997. Successful intelligence. New York: Plume.

———. 1998. Principles of teaching for successful intelligence. Educational Psychologist 33:65-72.

Stevenson, Harold, Max Lummis, Shin-Yin Lee, and James Stigler. 1990. Making the grade in mathematics. Arlington, VA: National Council of Teachers of Mathematics.

Stigler, James, and James Hiebert. 1998. Teaching is a cultural activity. American Educator 22 (4):4-11.

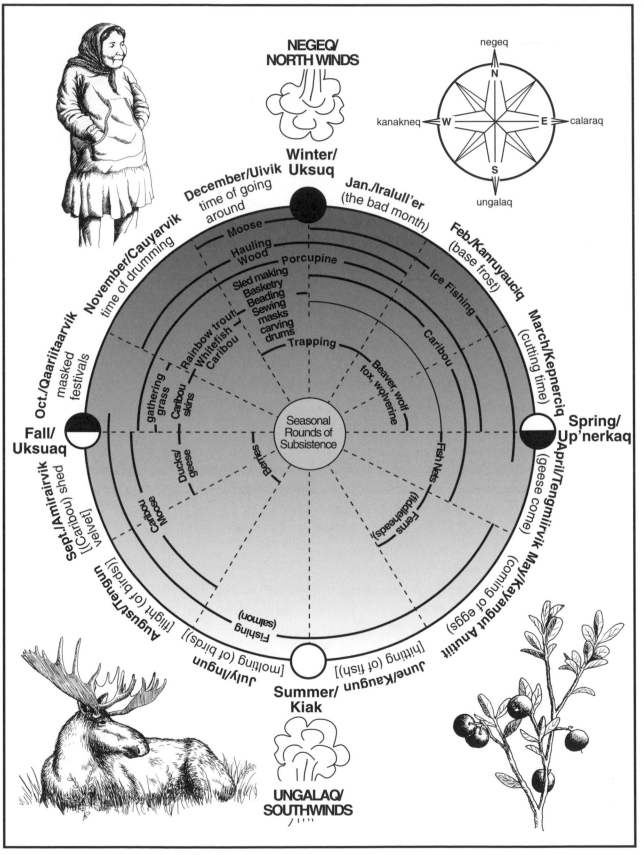

Fig. i: Yearly subsistence calendar

Patterns and
Introduction to the

Students working on the *Patterns and Parkas* module will discover

* how one shape can be decomposed into others;

* how designs can be put together to make patterns;

* how the Yup'ik people use geometry in their everyday lives; and

* how the fundamental concepts of geometry, symmetry, patterns, and spatial sense enable us to interpret and reflect on our physical environment.

Introduction to the Module

One of the most powerful uses of mathematics is the modeling of phenomena. Each person's concepts and skills in the areas of patterns and sequences grow in complexity over the years. Students' reasoning in geometry evolves and matures as they progress through school, allowing them to make increasingly complex mathematical representations. The Yup'ik Eskimo elders of southwest Alaska have developed superb fine motor skills and perception of precise angles, along with pattern and sequencing abilities that enable them to see symmetry and structure, helping them create art and the tools for living. Yup'ik knowledge of geometry is learned by careful observation, practice, investigation and attention to detail. The mathematical ideas and knowledge developed by the Yup'ik people are different in emphasis from, but similar in foundation to, those of school mathematics. Through experiences related to these Yup'ik skills, students improve their visual conceptualization and their abilities to describe, represent, classify, transform, and investigate space. Knowledge concerning mathematical concepts such as patterns, direction, and change enables the Yup'ik people to survive the extreme conditions in which they live. For example, Yup'ik sense of direction enables a person to find the way home during a whiteout, cross the tundra where no street signs exist, to find fish where no radar is available, and to create beautiful patterns without compass or ruler. This module provides students with some understandings of Yup'ik ways of organizing space as well as of school mathematics.

Always Getting Ready (*Upterrlainaryaraq*)

Always getting ready (*upterrlainaryaraq*) is not just a Yup'ik word, but is a way of life. The harsh climate mandates being ready for any activity—fishing, berry picking, sewing, a potlatch, a walk to school. Yup'ik men and women have always had to take care of themselves and construct the things they need for living: tools, shelters, toys, and clothing, everything that is necessary in the village. For years, Yup'ik Eskimo women have been cutting and sewing clothing for members of their families. They make dresses (*qasperet*), overcoats (*atkuut*), pants (*ulrut*), and warm boots (*piluguut*) (see Figure 1), without reliance on precut or predesigned patterns or measuring devices. They carefully observe the intended wearer, plan the design, visualize the proportions, cut the material, and sew it together into a garment that fits perfectly. They call this *tumartat*, "the putting together of pieces to form a whole." This module is about using pieces to understand shapes, area relationships, and to construct patterns.

Walkie Charles, a professor at the University of Alaska Fairbanks' Alaska Native Language Center whose home village is Emmonak in southwest Alaska, says:

> Tumartat is the gathering of pieces of anything and putting them together to make a whole. We look at what we sew—pieces of different types of furs, for instance—and we put them together to create one whole. We look at our patterns, different shapes are made and sewn together to create a whole. Everything around us is a pattern that creates our whole being. People have learned that they can *tumarciq* (put pieces together to make patterns) using shapes from their own surroundings and creating patterns that represent different aspects of their environment such as the animals, the mountains,

Fig. 1: Warm boots

and the stars. The representations of these shapes are commonly used to adorn clothing and tools. Designs are created for different cultural celebrations: mountains on headdresses and animals on women's dance fans. All of these are *tumartat*, the putting together of pieces to create a whole.

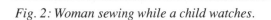

Fig. 2: Woman sewing while a child watches.

Mary Active, a Yup'ik elder from Togiak, Alaska, describes how she started sewing when she was very young.

I started to try to make dolls using a little piece of cloth. I was made to make them myself, and they began to improve. And I began to make parkas [winter coat typically with a hood and fur trim] for them and the parkas began to improve. I got faster in making them. I was probably ten when I started to make little boots for real babies and when I was 12 my mother had me make a pair of adult boots. She had me tan caribou legs and make a pair for Willie Coupchiak. . . The skin I tanned was probably tough . . . My mother told me that when she died she wasn't going to come back from the graveyard and show me how to sew and that I had to try to make them myself. So I tried very hard to sew by myself even though I would get very frustrated. Annie [her friend] and I would tell stories with our story knives, and when we got tired of that we'd go inside and make dolls and parkas for them. [Translation]

Note: Most of the information gathered for this module came from working with Yup'ik elders, so most quotations throughout this module have been translated into English from the original Yup'ik by project translators, and are marked as translations. Quotations concerning Yup'ik culture that are not marked as translations are from bilingual Yup'ik teachers who provided information in English.

Without the use of rulers or similar tools, Yup'ik women devise decorative borders for parkas and for fur boots (*mukluks*), consisting of a repeated motif of geometric shapes or more intricate figures. With the basic square as a foundation, women make isosceles right triangles, rectangles, parallelograms, smaller squares, and other shapes, while preserving specific size relationships to the original square and to the item they intend to decorate. These pieces are carefully cut from irregular-shaped skins and sewn together. Then the border is attached to the body of the parka. Again, this is called *tumartat*, "the putting together of pieces to form a whole."

In this module, students will learn how the Yup'ik people create patterns and make parkas. Students will be challenged to create patterns of their own and to use those patterns to create decorations for bookmarks, booklets, a classroom wall decoration, parka borders, and parkas with ruffs. They will engage in *tumartat*.

Mathematics Concepts

This module bases the development of plane geometric concepts on Yup'ik practices by drawing on the mathematical skills inherent in the culture. The Yup'ik people have developed visual conceptualization and estimation to a very high degree. They use multiple problem solving strategies, critical thinking skills, and complex reasoning.

When designing pattern pieces for linear designs, many elders start from a basic shape such as a square, rectangle, or rhombus and then make all other pieces related to the starting piece. This is the "genius" from a design and pedagogical point of view. Teaching students with these simple yet powerful and versatile tools allows students to explore:

- geometrical relationships;
- properties of shapes, including squares, rectangles, right isosceles triangles, and parallelograms;
- lines of symmetry;
- congruent shapes;
- linear repeating patterns;
- conjectures and proofs;
- conservation of area;
- part-to-part and part-to-whole relationships (fractions);
- measuring; and
- partitioning units or space.

In this module, the starting piece is the square. All other pieces made from the starting piece open up explorations into geometrical properties and relationships. Following the example of how Yup'ik elders create pattern pieces for parkas, students fold or cut a square. By partitioning the original square, students then develop pieces which are proportional to each other and are a fraction of the whole. These non-numeric investigations into part-to-whole relationships can form an intuitive and conceptual foundation for understanding fractions and area. This spatial approach to math follows the lead of others who suggest that teaching through spatial and visual modalities prior to numeric relationships (Harris, 1991) may make more sense to students who have considerable experience with spatial tasks.

James and James (1968), in their classic *Mathematics Dictionary*, define mathematics as "the logical study of shape, arrangement, quantity, and related concepts" (p. 226). They speak further of the purely mathematical concepts of space and number. The Yup'ik people use shape, arrangement, space, quantity, and number extensively and creatively in many ways, including the design and construction of border patterns and other types of decoration. The geometry in this module encourages children to recognize, describe, and record the properties, symmetries and relationships of squares and of shapes derived from the square. They also work on decomposition and recomposition of shapes to create basic repeating units; they describe and construct continuous repeating patterns. As they cut shapes apart and investigate part-whole relationships, they gain insights into conservation and measurement of area. Conjecturing, problem solving, offering proofs, formal and informal measurement, partitioning, and basic fraction concepts are introduced as students create their pattern designs. These activities prepare students for later work in geometry, including symmetry and uses in mathematical modeling.

The skills and knowledge developed by these activities are directly related to the precepts of the NCTM Curriculum and Evaluation Standards. Children are not regarded as "passive receivers of rules and procedures" but rather as "active participants in creating knowledge" (National Council of Teachers of Mathematics, 2000). Most of the activities incorporate the following standards for grades K-2: problem solving, communication, reasoning, estimation, number sense, whole number computation, geometry and spatial sense, measurement, and patterns and relationships. Connections are made between mathematical topics, as well as to other areas of the curriculum (art, language arts, science, social studies), and to the children's own environment.

Properties of Quadrilaterals

The module starts with a very familiar shape, a square. Most of us know that a square is a four-sided figure with four 90-degree angles (also called right angles) and four equal sides. As a consequence of these basic properties, the opposite sides of a square are parallel, and it possesses four lines of symmetry (one horizontal, one vertical, and two diagonal) as shown in Figure 3.

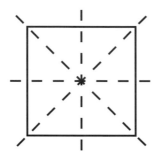

Fig. 3: Square showing lines of symmetry

A line of symmetry divides a figure into two equal parts in such a way that when the figure is folded along that line, the folded sides match each other perfectly. Yup'ik people use these properties—four right angles, all sides equal, four lines of symmetry—in order to construct squares from larger pieces of material. You can think of a square as a special kind of rectangle with all sides equal. As a result, a square includes the properties of a rectangle. The square and the rectangle are also special cases of a parallelogram, a quadrilateral with opposite sides equal and parallel and opposite angles equal. Figure 4 outlines the properties of those shapes.

Properties of a parallelogram	Properties of a rectangle	Properties of a square
• Four sides • Opposite sides equal and parallel • Opposite angles equal • No lines of symmetry	• Four sides • Opposite sides equal and parallel • All angles equal to 90 degrees • Two lines of symmetry passing through midpoints of sides	• Four sides • All sides equal and opposite sides parallel • All angles equal to 90 degrees • Four lines of symmetry passing through the midpoints of sides and the angle bisectors

Fig. 4: Properties of parallelogram, rectangle, and square

The figure below shows schematically how these special quadrilaterals are related.

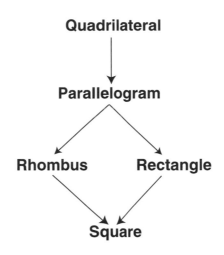

Fig. 5: Family of quadrilaterals

Squares and rectangles can also be divided into smaller congruent squares and rectangles. The simplest way is to fold and cut the original shape along its horizontal and vertical lines of symmetry to make four smaller shapes, each one-quarter of the area of the original square or rectangle.

Some Yup'ik parka designers divide squares and rectangles into three congruent parts by folding the original shape into thirds and cutting it. The folding is done by trial and error: the person folding must be careful to make sure all three sections are equal before making the final cuts. After a square has been divided equally into three rectangles, each of the rectangles can also be folded in thirds, to make three smaller congruent shapes—squares—each one-ninth the area of the original square, as shown in Figure 6.

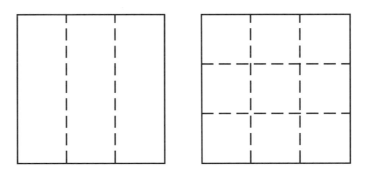

Fig. 6: A square folded into three equal rectangles in both directions,
creating nine congruent smaller squares

Properties of Right Isosceles Triangles

When you cut a square in half along one of its diagonals, the resulting triangles are right isosceles triangles, sometimes called half-square triangles. These have two equal sides with a 90-degree angle between them. The other two angles each equal 45 degrees. (See Figure 7) A right isosceles triangle has one line of symmetry, with the very nice property that if you fold and cut along this line you create two smaller congruent right isosceles triangles. You may continue this process, folding and cutting, to make smaller and smaller right isosceles triangles.

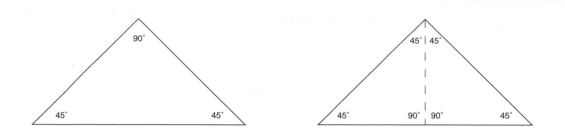

*Fig. 7: A right isosceles triangle divided along its line of symmetry
into two smaller right isosceles triangles*

There is one more proportional shape derived from squares that is used in some traditional Yup'ik patterns. This is a parallelogram made by dividing a square into two congruent triangles, then connecting the opposite edges to form a quadrilateral with opposite sides parallel. (See Figure 8) This parallelogram covers the same total area as the original square.

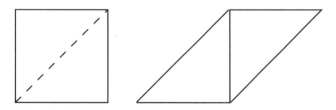

*Fig. 8: A parallelogram can be formed by cutting a square along one
of its diagonals and connecting the triangles along any of
their shorter edges.*

This basic set of shapes, all derived from squares and rectangles, makes up patterns that Yup'ik people put together in unique ways. *Tumaqcat* is the Yup'ik word for "putting together," and in this module we also use this word to refer to the unique pattern set. The figure below shows a sample of some possible *tumaqcat* shapes that can be derived from squares, maintaining the same area of the original square.

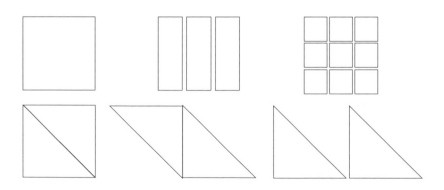

Fig. 9: Tumaqcat *pieces, putting together basic shapes from a square*

Math Note

Yup'ik designers cut all the shapes used for a particular pattern from a starting shape such as a basic square of the correct size. This approach illustrates three important geometric principles used in Yup'ik mathematical designs.

1. Take advantage of symmetry and congruence. By folding a square in half along a diagonal, the designer ensures that the resulting triangles will have a single line of symmetry and that the two right triangles will be congruent. Folding these triangles in half produces four congruent right triangles. Folding a square into thirds produces three congruent rectangles.
2. Create shapes whose edges match. The edges of the right triangles, rectangles, and squares produced by these methods will match up exactly. When they are made in different colors, they can be used to form patterns. This is an essential concept when sewing the pieces together.
3. Divide shapes in ways that preserve geometric relationships. Yup'ik designs frequently contain shapes whose areas are related by simple ratios. The area of a right isosceles triangle is ½ that of the basic square. If four right isosceles triangles are arranged to form a square, each has ¼ the area of the square. Similarly,

Investigating Area and Part-Whole Relationships

Area is defined as the amount of surface covered by a shape, measured in square units appropriate for the size of the region being measured. For example, square inches are used to measure a piece of paper, square yards for a rug, square miles for a city or state. In this module students explore area intuitively and by dividing shapes into congruent pieces and putting them together again.

Conservation of Area

Conservation of area is the concept underlying the development of all area concepts. In its simplest form it means that if you take any shape and subdivide it, the total area of all the pieces is the same as the original shape. Although this seems to be simple common sense, young children may have to verify this for themselves by recombining shapes into their original form, as shown in the figure below.

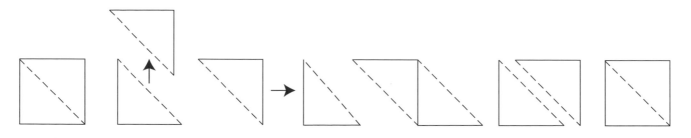

Fig. 10: Cutting a square into parts and making a parallelogram then putting the parts back together to make a square to illustrate the conservation of area.

Comparing Areas

The simplest area measurements in this unit involve comparing the areas of related shapes. Using their starting square, students will decompose and recompose that shape. The area remains constant but the visual image of the recomposed shape may no longer resemble the original square, challenging students' conception of conservation of area. Throughout the module students will grapple with this concept.

Parts and Wholes

The study of area comparisons also connects naturally to the study of parts and wholes (in other words, fractions). We've already seen an example showing that the area of a smaller square can be one-ninth the area of the square it was cut from. Students may already understand intuitively the relationships among different pieces of their pattern set and how they are related to other pieces and to the whole. This lays a good foundation for understanding fractions and potentially proportional thinking. Similarly dividing a square into two, four, and eight parts relates to numeration (repeated addition, multiplication, and division).

Combining Shapes to Make Patterns

The shapes derived from squares can be fit together in several ways, allowing a person to create many different patterns using the same basic shapes. Yup'ik pattern makers use squares, rectangles, and triangles in different sizes as well to create a variety of interesting linear patterns. Using shapes of two contrasting colors, usually black and white, they produce visually pleasing effects. The shapes derived from squares can be fit together in several different ways. This allows people to make many different patterns using the same basic shapes. A few examples are shown in Figures 11 and 12.

Yup'ik Pattern Pieces (*Tumaqcat*)

Yup'ik elders agreed on the word *tumartat* as "putting together pieces to make a whole." For this module, the Yup'ik pattern pieces are referred to as *tumaqcat* and are used to make patterns. The *tumaqcat* are based on some of the plane geometric shapes commonly used to form the repeating patterns on parkas and other decorated objects. These are not the only shapes found in border patterns, because different patterns are used in different areas.

Linear Patterns and Basic Repeating Units

Yup'ik designers use linear patterns for parka borders (bottom edge and sleeve cuffs), headbands, and fur boots (*mukluks*). These patterns all follow a few simple rules:

*   Start with a basic combination of shapes in contrasting colors. This becomes the basic repeating unit.
*   Copy that unit as many times as needed, in a linear sequence, to complete the pattern. (Combinations are usually arranged so that shapes line up edge to edge.)
*   Each pattern has a "balance point" at the center, with an equal number of design elements on either side. In a parka's bottom border, the balance point is at the center.
*   Usually (but not always) the balance point is a line of symmetry for the entire shape.

Fig. 11: Sample pattern strips designed according to Yup'ik principles.
(The balance point is shown as a dotted line.)

Throughout the module, students analyze existing patterns in order to identify the basic repeating units. By observing how these units fit together, they also learn how to construct linear patterns from basic elements. These experiences will help students understand patterns they see everywhere in the world around them. Repeating patterns of one, two, and three dimensions, as well as repeating rotational patterns, are found throughout the natural world, the constructed world, and the artistic world in which students live and grow up.

Mathematically, a repeating linear pattern could continue forever. However, in practice, a pattern has a beginning and an ending edge. These edges are constructed from only part of the basic repeating unit in order to end with a vertical edge. The "pretend windows" pattern in Figure 12(b) uses three copies of the basic repeating element and to make the edges square, the basic element is cut off at each end. The "pretend mountains" pattern in Figure 12(d) uses three complete repeats of the basic repeating element, and is cut off at each end similar to the first pattern. (You can visualize that half of a white triangle from the basic repeating element has been cut

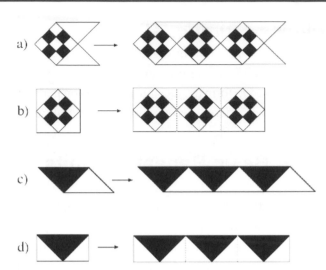

a) →

b) →

c) →

d) →

off one end and placed at the other.) You could think of the basic repeating element for the "pretend mountains" pattern containing the whole dark triangle with two smaller white triangles on each side. In this fashion, it's easy to see that unit repeated four times with an automatic beginning and ending edge. However, in practice an elder usually does not cut two small white triangles to sew together into a larger white triangle, thus the basic repeating element shown in Figure 12(c) is aligned with the practical.

Fig. 12: Basic repeating units to make patterns. Figure (a) shows the basic unit for pretend windows, while (b) shows another unit that can be used to create the repeated pattern. Figure (c) shows the basic unit for pretend mountains, while (d) shows another unit that can b e used to create the repeated pattern.

Estimation, Measurement, and Partitioning

Most Yup'ik pattern strips are designed to go around a parka's bottom edge or its sleeve cuffs. The parka designers plan carefully so that as the pattern completes the circle the two ends match, giving the sense of a pattern that continues forever.

A parka designer must consider the following questions: How big should the starting squares or rectangles be? How many pieces of each type will I need to complete my pattern? How can I ensure that when all the pieces are cut and sewn, the pattern will "close" perfectly as it circles the bottom of the parka?

Fig. 13: A parka using the pretend windows pattern

Look at the parka in Figure 13. You can tell these are not trivial questions to answer. You can also see that the same basic pattern element is used, in a shorter length, to circle the cuffs of the parka.

The task of determining how many repeating elements can fit within a given pattern, and how large they should be, is called partitioning. Yup'ik parka designers partition their borders intuitively, without actually measuring. Because they have made and seen many parkas of different sizes, they know from experience that they will need to start with a basic shape of a particular size to fit a parka border of particular height and length.

First they decide on the height of the border strip; this is often measured using fingers. A strip could be two, three, or four fingers high depending on the size of the garment and the designer's taste. Once the height is determined, the size of the basic shape, usually a square or rectangle, is also determined.

While Yup'ik elders do not rely on such methods for measuring, a conventional mathematical way to partition a parka border into equal-sized parts is to use a measuring tape and standard measures. First measure the distance around the bottom of the parka. Next decide on the height of the strip. This will determine the size of your *tumaqcat* pieces. (In the pretend windows pattern, the height of the strip is the diagonal distance across the large square from which all the small black and white squares and the white right isosceles triangles are cut.) Once you know the height, you can determine the length of the basic repeating unit.

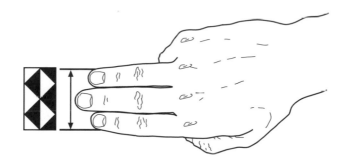

Fig. 14: This border strip is three fingers wide

Measure the length of the repeating unit and divide that into the length of the border. If this does not come out to be a whole number, you'll probably want to increase or decrease the size of your basic pattern element slightly, to make a slightly wider or narrower band, so that you will be able to complete the pattern without overlap. If you were to start making a parka border without doing this partitioning you might be very disappointed to find that your pattern no longer maintains the basic unit.

After you know the number of repeating elements you can calculate the total number of pieces needed.

Students confront the partitioning problem during the module when they make their own patterns. One way to help students work this out is to have them cut a strip of the length needed, and then repeatedly folding it in half, dividing it into small, equal sections. This is an intuitive method of partitioning a strip into equal segments that determine the size of the repeating elements.

Measuring with Nonstandard Units

Students also use objects of nonstandard units, such as bookmarks, to measure objects in the classroom. Accurate measurement of a long distance with a short object is a skill that may take some time for your students to develop. It is best carried out in pairs. One important subskill is marking where the object ends (using a mark or a finger), then shifting the object so it begins again at that spot. A second subskill is keeping count of the number of times the object length has been repeated.

If the total length is not equal to an exact number of object lengths, a third subskill is accounting for the remaining partial length of the object using fractional measures, or smaller units, that are subdivisions of the object.

When a nonstandard ruler such as a bookmark is used, the length of a repeating element may provide a convenient way to subdivide the bookmark. In Figure 15 below, the distance to be measured is between three and four bookmark lengths. Since the bookmark is made up of seven repeats of a basic pattern element, the length being measured approximates $3\frac{4}{7}$ bookmark lengths.

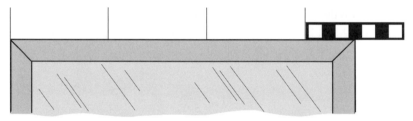

Fig. 15: Measuring a length using a bookmark divided into smaller units

If the bookmark cannot easily be divided into smaller units, students may prefer to approximate a length to the nearest half-bookmark length. In Figure 15 above, the length could be expressed as approximately $3\frac{1}{2}$ bookmark lengths.

Another approach is to make another strip the length of the bookmark and fold it in half, and in half again to divide it into quarters, and once more to make eighths.

Mathematical Reasoning: Conjecture and Proof

In addition to the practical problem solving involved in this module, students are sometimes asked to prove whether a certain statement is true or not. This is a big step in developing mathematical understanding and is a basic component of all mathematical thinking.

Mathematical investigations often take the following form:
• You observe a certain situation and look for patterns.
• When you think you've found a pattern, you make a conjecture, that is, a statement about a mathematical fact, relationship, or generalization that is based on careful observation or experimentation but which has not been proven.
• You try to prove your conjecture using previously known facts and logical systems of reasoning.

In this module, students make a type of conjecture when they first construct their squares. Once they have cut out what they think is a square, they can prove whether or not it is a valid square by folding it in half along lines of symmetry to check if all the sides match up. They are using known facts—that a square has four equal sides, along with the other properties of a square—to prove whether or not the shape they have constructed is a square.

Another type of conjecture involves comparing the areas of different pieces. This is important for determining the amount of material needed to construct a pattern. For instance, in the "pretend windows" pattern, students may want to decide how many squares they will need in order to cut their pieces. A student may make a conjecture that the two white triangles could be cut from a single square, the size of the pattern's "checkerboard" square (see Figure 16). They could verify this conjecture by cutting out two triangles of the same size. If they fit exactly on top of the square, that would represent a proof of the conjecture.

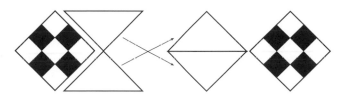

Fig. 16: The white triangles in the "pretend windows" pattern, when paired, are equal in size to the "checkerboard" square in the pattern.

These ways of proving geometric facts and relationships provide a foundation for proof at a level accessible to second graders. Though not as rigorous as the formal proofs used by mathematicians, they do satisfy the criteria for proof because they are based on known properties and logical reasoning.

Pedagogy of the Module

Mary Active, an elder from Togiak, Alaska, explained how she learned to sew:

> Before we started to make dolls we used to story knife… Drawing people and things that we would make in the future. We [did make] dolls, and later on parkas for dolls. Before I began to sew, I used to watch my mother and then later on she would put the skin side out and make me patch the holes on the parka. When I first started patching the holes, my sewing wasn't that good. They'd (stitches would) be crooked or one side would be too long even though I tried my best. As time went by they got better and better. They were no longer crooked or too long on one side. I learned that that was how it was for all children. When they first start, their stitches are very bad. (Translation)

Years ago one of the authors had the opportunity to observe Evelyn Yanez, a consultant to MCC and a retired teacher from Togiak, Alaska, use expert-apprentice modeling as part of her classroom teaching (Lipka and Yanez, 1998). She demonstrated a task and had the students observe her, similar to the way Mary Active described how she learned as a young girl. However, schooling is not the community and Ms Yanez had a classroom of students under her supervision. She adapted the expert-apprentice model by having more experienced and more attentive students demonstrate to other students until all of the students were productively engaged. Similarly, within this module, students will have an opportunity to practice experiential learning. Students will begin by observing an elder, or teacher, or use the included DVD, *Tumartat: Putting the Pieces Together to Make a Whole* that shows elders cutting and making squares from a sheet of irregular material and making a design using the square and other pieces made from the square. Elders are also shown making squares in other ways as well as making rhombi.

Further, while observing Nancy Sharp, a teacher from Manokotak, Alaska, make designs while teaching this module we noticed how she extended expert-apprentice modeling to include joint productive activity and cognitive apprenticeship. She worked in parallel with the students (joint productive activity) as well as demonstrated for her students. When she faced problems and challenges she used these as opportunities to talk aloud and explain the problem and what she might do. Sharp's and Yanez's ways of organizing the classroom profoundly affected the interactions between the teacher and student creating a classroom that appeared to be harmonious—students and teachers working together for a common purpose (Lipka, Sharp, Brenner, Yanez, and Sharp, 2005). Nancy Sharp then challenged her students to make squares from irregular material, produce designs, and create their own patterns. Although she used expert-apprentice modeling she also fostered students' creativity as students produced a diverse set of patterns.

MCC encourages use of small cooperative groups as students solve the problems inherent in the task. When working in groups, children often model for each other, working together so everyone learns. As they create various patterns, the students discover the attributes of squares, rectangles, triangles, and parallelograms by observing actual patterns and cutting the shapes necessary to reproduce them. As they plan their own repeated border patterns, students hone their skills in computation, estimation, and spatial visualization.

In this module, each student creates an original repeating border pattern based on geometric shapes. Students have the opportunity to work with a specially designed set of Yup'ik pattern pieces (*tumaqcat*) based on the geometric shapes and relationships found in the repeating patterns on parka borders, fur boots (*mukluks*), and other clothing and tools made by the Yup'ik people.

Teacher as Elder in the Classroom

When the module is used, an elder can be invited to demonstrate and explain the work he or she is doing while the students observe, practice, and learn. Invite parents to accompany the elder so modeling may be continued at home. Where no elder is available, the teacher or the DVD functions as the elder, modeling ways of teaching and learning. The DVD includes the following lessons: Folding a Perfect Square, Making a Strip of Squares, Making Squares, Square to Circle, Rectangle to Rhombus, Rectangle to Fancy Rhombus, and Square to Parallelogram. For more details, see page 30.

The elder (or teacher) creates something he or she needs and wants to make, for instance, a set of squares that are to be part of a border pattern. The children observe and attempt to duplicate the work. They talk with each other and model for those having difficulty. If some students return to the elder to observe further, the elder continues the work, allowing the students to watch. Then the students go back to their own work, to struggle again with the concept. The children learn by observing the elder, by observing each other, and by trying to create the patterns and pieces themselves. When Anuska Nanalook, an elder from Manokotak, Alaska, was asked what she would do when a child had difficulty, she replied: "If the child wanted help, I would model it for him." (Translation)

Another interesting technique used by the elders and by some Yup'ik teachers is to start teaching whomever is there, rather than waiting for a whole group to assemble. The teacher shows a few students—those who have arrived—what to do and then expects those students to show others as they come in. The students are responsible for imparting knowledge to their classmates, which requires enough understanding to be able to repeat the work for other students.

It is not the Yup'ik way to ask direct questions to which one already knows the answer. Direct questions appear invasive and do not convey respect. *Apqaussiiyaagpeknak*, don't ask so many questions, represents respect in the Yup'ik culture. Preserving this cultural value in the classroom setting makes assessment difficult, so the transition to Western ways comes quickly in that aspect of the module. However, the decision as to how and when to ask questions is the professional responsibility of the teacher. Many teachers find the embedded assessment modeled here—with questions asked of individuals or small groups while they are working—to be helpful in determining whether or not lesson objectives are met as well as in planning subsequent work.

No attempt is made in this module to repeat classroom dialogue. It is expected that the teacher will validate children's statements. Even a completely wrong answer can be used sensitively to encourage children's thinking. Discussion where children disagree with each other can be stimulating and productive.

Patterns in Other Cultures

Throughout the world, people have created complex patterns for utility and beauty. Anthropology researchers have found one-dimensional and two-dimensional patterns in many cultures. Anthropologists today use the symmetries found in such patterns as a tool in classifying objects and tracing their origins (Washburn and Crowe, 1988). The Spanish Moors are famous for their intricately patterned mosaics in the Alhambra; the Pueblos of the southwest United States create patterned pottery that brings international acclaim; and the Amish people's making of quilts is certainly an example of the putting pieces together to create a whole. In her novel, *How to Make an American Quilt*, Whitney Otto writes:

> What you should understand when undertaking the construction of a quilt is that it is comprised of spare time as well as excess material. . . . It utilizes that which would normally be thrown out, "waste," and eliminates the extra, the scraps. And out of that which is left comes a new, useful object. . . . The fairly intricate quilt will contain, roughly, thirty-five pieces per block. Perhaps a thousand pieces in a finished quilt. Shake your head in amazement at the occasional quilt that boasts thousands of pieces. Puzzle out the fact that a single woman could hold all those pieces together without misplacing, losing, or mistaking a piece. Understand that she must be someone of extraordinary strength and organization and discipline. (Otto, 1991, pp. 9, 37)

Using the *Patterns and Parkas* Module

The *Patterns and Parkas* module consists of three parts, with a total of six activities and two projects. The projects consolidate the mathematics learned through each activity. Each activity connects math to the Yup'ik culture. The four explorations connect the Yup'ik culture to the math of the module.

- The Introduction to the Module is an overview of the module and is intended to supply information for teachers to share with students about Yup'ik culture and Yup'ik ways of knowing and learning. The traditional process of learning through observation and practice is central to the module. Background and historical information about symmetry in patterns is included, and mathematical concepts are briefly discussed. The activities are the heart of this module, and they are extended classroom math experiences based on information from the elders regarding Yup'ik culture.

- Section 1: Putting the Pieces Together to Make a Whole (*Tumartat*), sets the tone for the entire module through hands-on experience of making a square in Activity 1. Students make a square from uneven paper. As they do this they learn about the properties of a square. Students learn other methods of making a square and they learn to use symmetry in this process. Further, they learn how to distinguish a square from a rectangle. Activity 2 leads students to discover the relationship between the square and other geometrical shapes. Shapes that are typically used in *tumartat*. More specifically, students learn to make different shapes from a square: right triangles, parallelograms, and a rectangles by decomposing a square and reassembling the pieces into different shapes. Students explore dividing a square into congruent shapes. To consolidate their knowledge about different shapes, how they are related and how they are different, students practice sorting and classifying shapes. Activity 3 introduces the repetition and creation of patterns. Also, this activity introduces students to scaling.The students become involved in their first project. Projects are designed to integrate students' developing mathematical knowledge. Projects have mathematical, cultural, and practical components. In the first project students make a bookmark. Later the bookmark serves as a ruler. In activity 4 students use their bookmarks as a ruler. This forces them to pay attention to their basic unit. They explore issues related to measuring such as the concept of repeated units, partial units, and how you count units. This lesson relates to the next project which occurs in Activity 6 when students will measure objects in the room that they will decorate. In activity 5 students identify the basic repeating unit in the bookmarks they made in activity 3. Activity 6 includes a second project as students make a decorative border pattern for the classroom. This is one of a series of culminating activities. Students apply what they learned about making patterns, symmetry, measuring, and repeating units. Simultaneously, this activity is coordinated with Explorations A-D where these skills are applied to a Yup'ik parka border pattern.

- Section 2, Explorations A–D, Making a Parka (*Atkuk*) is a stand-alone section intended to run parallel to the math activities. Time outside of math class is devoted to constructing the parka. The pieces are brought-together to make a whole (tumartat) as students construct a paper parka and add the ruff, the tassels, and the borders. This section of the module should be completed by the time you finish the math activities. The border patterns created in Activity 6 may be added last. Through exploration, observation, and practice, students learn about the shapes used in *tumaqcat* (the putting together of pattern pieces), and the relationship between size, area, and symmetry among the individual pieces. The section demonstrates the Yup'ik idea that we can all make patterns (*tumarciyugngaukut*). Students create a math notebook that includes their collection of traditional border patterns and unique individual patterns. Additional activities expanding on previous learning challenge students to think and apply the knowledge they have gained through observation and practice.

The module also includes a powerful teaching tool, a DVD titled Tumartat: Putting the Pieces Together to Make a Whole. This DVD assists with understanding the Yup'ik culture, particularly how elders make patterns, and how those processes to connect to the math of the module. The table of contents is listed on page 30.

Literacy Counts: Developing Language and Literacy in MCC

Literacy Counts is a supplemental literacy guide designed to accompany MCC. As MCC has developed over the years, the importance of the role of literacy has also grown. The inclusion of culturally based stories has proven to contribute to students' engagement with the math modules while providing cultural grounding for the module activities. MCC modules have also made use of literacy-based activities, such as journaling, to further students' understanding of math concepts and vocabulary. Building on these trends and practices, we have developed Literacy Counts.

There are two strands within the Literacy Counts approach: (a) Strand 1, designed to develop literacy in the traditional linguistic modes (speaking, writing, reading, listening, and presenting), as well as in other nonlinguistic modes (two-dimensional drawings or three-dimensional models), in order to communicate mathematically and practice mathematics; and (b) Strand 2, designed to develop multiple literacies (linguistic, visual, kinesthetic, spatial, etc.) through the use of culturally relevant stories and nonfiction literature that accompany MCC modules.

In this module, literacy connects through an accompanying story, *Iluvaktuq*, about a legendary Yup'ik warrior. (His existence is corroborated by Russian journals, and some modern-day Yupiaq parkas include symbols that denote direct familial relationship to Iluvaktuq.) This second-grade read-aloud storybook can be obtained from the publisher.

Assessment

In observing the teaching methods of Yup'ik elders and hearing them discuss their own experiences, it became clear to us that their respect for others, young or old, is a vital part of their process. They teach by example, making something they themselves want, and they teach when the child feels ready to learn. They observe progress but do not compare one student's progress to that of others. Learning and doing are the important parts.

"The purpose of assessment should be to improve learning," wrote Jean Stenmark in *Assessment Alternatives in Mathematics*. She advised that we should expand the ways in which students can demonstrate their mathematical achievements, as well as the ways teachers can gain better information about their students' learning.

> This way . . . there will be less need for complex scoring and grading of student work. Comparing students will become less important than helping students understand mathematics. (Stenmark, 1989, p. 4)

Assessment should be integral to instruction and not detract from students' opportunities to continue to learn. The means of assessment should be as varied as the student products. In this module, student work from the problems, exercises, and activities can be collected for portfolios. Student math notebooks can be read and responses written. Photographs of students working are effective records of involvement and persistence. It is essential that students develop the ability to demonstrate that they understand the mathematical ideas involved, that they can handle non-routine problems, do original work, and that they understand relationships between practical work, classroom exercises, and abstract concepts. Completing a task is important, but doing a "good job" is also important. Willingness to practice and try again when self-evaluation deems it necessary is a life-long skill.

Most of the activities are appropriate as both learning experiences and assessment tools. It may be useful to carry a clipboard of students' names to record observations of students' learning as the work progresses. Also, examination of papers and artifacts created and turned in will provide information on students' learning.

Portfolios of the work students select are important records of student development. All classroom assessment should be used to help students develop skills and knowledge, rather than to categorize children on the basis of presumed "ability levels." Children differ in their skills and interests, and these activities are sufficiently varied to appeal to most children.

Useful Work

Children watch and learn from Yup'ik adults as these adults create useful items. Whatever is being made is created for a useful purpose, not simply in order to teach. This is readily apparent to all, and the importance of the learning is underscored by the value and usefulness the teacher places on making his or her item. The artifacts to be made in this module—bookmarks, classroom wall decorations, parka borders, and parkas—are all useful objects and thus reflect the spirit of the Yup'ik way of teaching.

Pattern and Parka Posters

The posters show some of the repeating patterns that make use of basic geometric shapes found on Yup'ik fur parkas. There are many other shapes that represent plants, birds, insects, and animals. Some parkas are also decorated with stitching or beading. Many of the geometric shapes have different meanings, depending on geographical area. In this module, we are using the shapes the elders we spoke with have seen and find familiar. They are not the only patterns or names for patterns. Marie Napoka, a teacher's aide from Tuluksak, Alaska, and the late Mary George of Akiachak, Alaska, first collected these pattern names and shapes from elders in their region.

Display the posters of pattern and parka examples in a high-use area of the classroom. For example, place them near the door where the students line up for transitional activities. Introduce the names of the repeating patterns in an informal way. The names can be introduced both in Yup'ik (using the CD-ROM), and in the English translations.

Ask the children to look at the first repeating pattern on the poster and talk about the pattern and the name. Find the same repeating pattern, pretend box (*yaassiiguaq*), on one of the parka posters. Continue with other patterns so the children will gradually become familiar with the illustrations on both posters. Have the children look for the patterns in other areas of the school, home, and community.

Materials Management

The manipulatives and materials for an activity should be readily available to students. A plastic container for each group of students, containing the common supplies used with many different activities, can be stored on a shelf so a volunteer from each group can bring it to the table. Thus, essentials such as colored markers, pencils, crayons, paste sticks, and scissors can be obtained quickly. The lids of copy-paper boxes make easy storage for the various sizes and types of paper to be used. Some teachers have substituted copy paper for construction paper, finding it easier for young students to fold and cut.

An overhead projector has many purposes in this module. Drawings, diagrams, and worksheets can be shown and explained on the overhead. Outlines of Yup'ik pattern pieces and other models of geometric shapes are projected clearly on it. If no overhead projector is available, use a felt board, chart paper, or the chalkboard as substitute devices. Using a mirrors or a MIRA© (a reflective device that demonstrates symmetry, rotation, flips, and movement) allows the students to see more clearly the symmetry of the shapes, basic repeating units, and patterns.

Large folders or envelopes for work in progress may help keep papers and products together until a project can be completed. Individual portfolios can be used to store each student's selected work from a unit. A large scrapbook can be used to save pictures and photographs that pertain to the class as a whole. Whenever possible, plan for volunteers to pass out and collect materials, leaving the teacher free to talk with individuals, ask questions, and ensure a good working atmosphere. Discuss the use of materials with the class, and elicit from them a few positive general guidelines for respectful use of materials and courteous treatment of one another. Emphasize the cultural aspect of not wasting materials and provide a way for the students to save their scraps for use in later activities.

Letter Home to the Family

When families are kept informed of what is happening at school, they are usually very supportive. A class discussion of the letter will help students tell their families about the module. The letter, in either English or Yup'ik, should be duplicated, signed, and sent home with each student at the beginning of this module. Many teachers choose to duplicate the Yup'ik on one side of the paper and the English on the other, equally valuing both languages.

Dear Student and Family:

In mathematics we are starting a series of activities that involve counting, sorting, recognizing shapes and patterns, discovering the properties of geometric shapes, working with lines of symmetry, and creating and identifying sequences. Students will learn about the mathematics inherent in Yup'ik culture while they strengthen their knowledge of school mathematics.

What are the expectations of students and families?

Students can expect to
- work in a group and contribute to accomplishing group tasks;
- organize their own work instead of being told exactly what to do;
- complete all assignments;
- produce individual work as well as group projects;
- demonstrate initiative, creativity, and mathematical knowledge.

How can families help?

- Take an interest in the work. Ask your child, "What are you working on in math class?" You will find out what we are doing, and your child will learn to put into words what he or she is learning. You may help your child with the mathematics if you wish, but be sure he or she understands any special techniques you use.
- Come to school when you can. The students would enjoy hearing of your experiences related to what we are doing.

Sincerely,

Mathematics Teacher

Elitnauraq, Angayuqaak-llu

Naaqut'liuryarami ayagnirtukut ayuqenrilngurnek caarkanek elitnaurutkamtenek. Ayagniqatartukut allakariyaramek, elucit ayuqenrilnguut elicarluki, kingukurluki-llu elliqcaaryaramek. Elitnaurat elitarkauluteng naaqut'liuryaramek aturluki Yugtun elicaraput taringekanircelluki naaqut'liuryaranek.

Caugat caarkait elitnaurat ilaita-llu?

Elitnaurat waten piciqut:

- Caliluteng quyurmeng;
- Ellmeggnek pingnaqluteng kia ikayunrilengraateng;
- Qaqiulluki caarkateng tamalkuita;
- Ellmeggnek caliluteng cali-llu allanek ilaluteng;
- Nasviitaariluteng naaqut'liuryaramek ayuqenrilngurteggun.

Qaillun nakmiin ilat ikayuuciiqat?

- Caliaritnek apqaurluki. Apyutkan irniavnun, "Canek elicarcit naaqut'liuryarami?" Nallunrirciquten canek elitellrinek irniarpet apqaullerpekun. Irniavet-llu qalarutekluki elitellni elpenun ikayuutnguciqluni elitekanillerkaanun elliin. Ikayuryugngaan irnian nallunrilkengavnek ikayurcetaaqan taugaam nallunritevkarluku qaillun pillerpenek.
- Taigaqluten elitnaurvigmun piyugngaaqavet. Elitnaurat quyaciqut nallunrilkengavnek nasviskuvki elitnaurviatni.

Quyana,

Naaqut'liuryaranek Elitnaurista

NCTM Standards and Math Goals of the Module

Principles and Standards for School Mathematics (2000)

Students in prekindergarten through grade 2 should be able to

Number and Operations Standard

- Understand numbers, ways of representing numbers, relationships among numbers, and number systems:
  - count with understanding and recognize "how many" in sets of objects;
  - connect number words and numerals to the quantities they represent, using various physical models and representations;
  - understand and represent commonly used fractions, such as ¼, ⅓, and ½.
- Compute fluently and make reasonable estimates:
  - use a variety of methods and tools to compute, including objects, mental computation, estimation, paper and pencil, and calculators.

Algebra Standard

- Understand patterns, relations and functions:
  - sort, classify, and order objects by size, number and other properties;
  - recognize, describe, and extend patterns such as sequences of sounds and shapes or simple numeric patterns and translate from one representation to another;
  - analyze how both repeating and growing patterns are generated.

Geometry Standard

- Analyze characteristics and properties of two-dimensional geometric shapes and develop mathematical arguments about geometric relationships:
  - recognize, name, build, compare and sort two-dimensional shapes;
  - describe attributes and parts of two-dimensional shapes;
  - investigate and predict the results of putting together and taking apart two-dimensional shapes.
- Apply transformations and use symmetry to analyze mathematical situations:
  - recognize and apply slides, flips and turns;
  - recognize and create shapes that have symmetry.
- Use visualization, spatial reasoning, and geometric modeling to solve problems:
  - create mental images of geometric shapes using spatial memory and spatial visualization;
  - recognize and represent shapes from different perspectives;
  - relate ideas in geometry to ideas in number and measurement;
  - recognize geometric shapes and structures in the environment and specify their location.

Measurement Standard

- Understand measurable attributes of objects and the units, systems, and process of measurement:
  - recognize the attributes of length and area;

- compare and order objects according to these attributes;
- understand how to measure using nonstandard units;
- select an appropriate unit and tool for the attribute being measured.

- Apply appropriate techniques, tools, and formulas to determine measurements:
  - measure with multiple copies of units of the same size, such as paper clips laid end to end;
  - use repetition of a single unit to measure something larger than the unit, for instance, measuring the length of the room with a single meter stick;
  - develop common referents for measures to make comparisons and estimates.

Problem Solving Standard

- Build new mathematical knowledge through problem solving.
- Solve problems that arise in mathematics and in other contexts.
- Apply and adapt a variety of appropriate strategies to solve problems.
- Monitor and reflect on the process of mathematical problem solving.

Reasoning and Proof Standard

- Recognize reasoning and proof as fundamental aspects of mathematics.
- Make and investigate mathematical conjectures.
- Develop and evaluate mathematical arguments and proofs.
- Select and use various types of reasoning and methods of proof.

Communication Standard

- Organize and consolidate their mathematical thinking through communication.
- Communicate their mathematical thinking coherently and clearly to peers, teachers, and others.
- Analyze and evaluate the mathematical thinking and strategies of others.
- Use the language of mathematics to express mathematical ideas precisely.

Connections Standard

- Recognize and use connections among mathematical ideas.
- Understand how mathematical ideas interconnect and build on one another to produce a coherent whole.
- Recognize and apply mathematics in contexts outside of mathematics.

Alaska Standards for Culturally Responsive Schools

(Alaska Native Knowledge Network, 1998)

A culturally responsive curriculum
- reinforces the integrity of the cultural knowledge that students bring with them;
- recognizes cultural knowledge as part of a living and constantly adapting system that is grounded in the past, but continues to grow through the present and into the future;

Master Vocabulary List

Angle—a geometric figure formed when two lines, rays, or line segments meet at a point. The meeting point is called the vertex of the angle. An angle is measured in degrees of rotation between the two lines, rays, or line segments.

Area—the amount of surface covered by a shape or region. Area is most often measured in square units appropriate to the size of the shape or region, such as square inches, square yards, square miles, and so forth.

Basic repeating unit—a shape or collection of shapes that, when repeatedly copied and moved, make up a pattern. Basic repeating unit refers to the smallest set of shapes that can be used to generate an entire pattern. (See Linear Pattern, Two-dimensional Pattern)

Center—a point that is equidistant from all points in a circle; a point that is equidistant from all sides of a regular polygon.

Concentric circles—a set of two or more circles that share a common center.

Congruence—the property of two shapes that are congruent.

Congruent—geometric figures (or parts of figures) that are the same shape and size. Two shapes are congruent if one shape can be slid, flipped, and/or rotated so that the shape fits exactly on top of the other one. Parts of a shape—for example, sides or angles—may also be congruent.

Conjecture—a statement about a mathematical fact, relationship, or generalization that is based on careful observation or experimentation but which has not been proven. (See Proof)

Conservation of area—when a shape is divided into two or more parts, all of the parts cover the same total area as the original shape.

Design—a pleasing shape or combination of shapes. A design may be intentionally created by someone or may be a consequence of natural forces.

Diagonal—a line segment opposite vertices of any quadrilateral.

Ellipse—the set of all points in a plane such that the sum of the distances to two fixed points is a constant. (See Oval)

Equilateral triangle—a triangle with all three sides the same length and all three angles equal to 60 degrees.

Estimation of length—making a reasoned guess of a length based on careful observation and prior experience.

Horizontal line—a line parallel to the ground. Horizontal and vertical lines meet at right angles.

Hypotenuse—the side opposite the right angle in a right triangle.

Isosceles triangle—a triangle with at least two sides the same length. The angles at the base of an isosceles triangle are also equal.

Linear pattern—a one-dimensional (potentially) infinite pattern which repeats a basic unit (geometric shape or design) over and over again, such as in a band, border pattern, or strip pattern. These are sometimes called "frieze patterns" because of their use in architectural settings.

Line segment—a part of a line with two endpoints and a definite length.

Line of symmetry—a line that is a property of a geometric figure (a shape, design, or pattern); it divides the figure into two equal parts such that when the figure is reflected about that line, the result is identical to the starting figure. For example, a square has four lines of symmetry: one vertical, one horizontal, and two diagonal lines through the center. An informal test for a line of symmetry in a two-dimensional shape is to fold the shape along a line through its center. If both sides match exactly after folding, the line is a line of symmetry.

Line symmetry—a property of a geometric figure that has one or more lines of symmetry. (See Mirror Symmetry)

Mirror symmetry—a property of a geometric figure with one or more lines of symmetry. If you place a mirror along a line of symmetry, the visual effect is that the half of the object and its reflection look exactly like the complete object.

Orientation—the property of a shape that describes its location in relation to its rotation from a reference line.

Oval—the everyday word for the math term "ellipse." You can think of an oval as an elongated circle.

Parallelogram—a quadrilateral with both pairs of opposite sides parallel and equal.

Pattern—a design that consists of a basic repeating unit repeated over and over again; a pattern may be extended in one direction (linear or frieze pattern), two directions (two-dimensional or "wallpaper" pattern), or three directions (crystal pattern).

Plane—a flat surface that extends infinitely in all directions. Mathematically, a plane is considered to have zero thickness and is two-dimensional with length and width.

Polygon—a simple closed curve made up of connected line segments or sides.

Proof—a mathematical argument, based on logical reasoning, that demonstrates that a particular fact or relationship is true. (See Conjecture)

Properties—the attributes of a geometric shape (sides, angles, symmetries and their relationships) that define a particular shape as a unique shape. For example, the basic properties of a square are that it has four equal sides and four equal angles. From these stem additional properties: its angles all equal 90 degrees, it has four lines of symmetry, and it is rotationally symmetrical when rotated 90 degrees about its center.

Quadrilateral—a four-sided polygon.

Rectangle—a quadrilateral with four equal angles, all equal to 90 degrees. Its opposite sides are parallel and equal to each other. Alternatively, a rectangle is a parallelogram with all angles equal.

Regular polygon—a polygon whose sides and angles are all equal. A square is a regular quadrilateral.

Repeating unit—a shape or collection of shapes that is repeated to make a linear pattern.

Right angle—an angle that measures 90 degrees, or one-fourth of a full rotation. This is the angle found in squares, rectangles and right triangles. It is sometimes called a "square angle."

Right isosceles triangle—a triangle that includes a right angle and two equal sides. A right isosceles triangle is sometimes called a "half-square triangle." It must have a 90-degree angle and two 45-degree angles.

Rotational symmetry—the quality of a geometric figure (shape, design, or pattern) such that when the figure is rotated about a given point, through a particular angle, the result is identical to the original shape. For example, when a square is rotated about its center through exactly 90 degrees, the result is identical to the square before it was rotated.

Ruler—a standardized tool used for measuring length.

Scaling—a nonrigid geometric transformation that shrinks or expands a geometric shape, so that every length in the shape is multiplied by the same ratio, called a "scale factor." Scaling affects only the length of a shape. Its angles are unchanged, and the relative proportions of one length to another are also unchanged.

Shape—form or outline.

Square—a regular quadrilateral. All sides have the same length and all the angles are right angles. Alternatively, a square is a rectangle with all sides the same length.

Symmetry—a quality of a shape such that the shape does not change when transformed by a rigid transformation. There are three types of symmetry: line symmetry (or mirror symmetry), rotational symmetry (or point symmetry), and translational symmetry.

Transformation—moving a shape using translation, rotation, and/or reflection, in such a way as to preserve the shape.

Translational symmetry—a property of a geometric figure such that the figure is repeated moving along a line in any direction.

Triangle—a polygon with three sides.

Two-dimensional pattern—a two-dimensional (potentially) infinite pattern which repeats a basic unit (geometric shape or design) over and over again. Two-dimensional patterns are sometimes referred to as "wallpaper patterns."

Unit of measure—a scale used to record measurements of length, area, temperature, etc.

Vertex, vertices—the point or points at which sides of a polygon, or lines of an angle meet. Vertices of polygons are sometimes called "corners."

Vertical line—a line perpendicular to the ground, or the bottom of a figure, or a piece of paper. Vertical and horizontal lines meet at right angles.

Glossary of Yup'ik Terms

Akunlengqerrluteng—pattern with something between the repeating shapes.

Alngailnguar—one without tassels.

Alngat—center front tassel.

Asguruaq—ruff; an oval shaped fur attached to a hood to protect the face and head from cold.

Atkuk—parka.

Ayuqlutek akiqliqellriik—pattern or design with opposite sides the same (symmetrical).

Ayuquralriit—repeating element in a pattern.

Cauyaruaq—pretend drum.

Cetumquruaq—bird claws.

Ciligtaq—something cut at an angle.

Ciligtellria yaassiigenqellria—square, tilted (a square turned at an angle).

Cuignilnguq—land or river otter.

Egaleruat—the base word is *egaleq–*, which means "window" (singular), and the ending *–uaq*, which means "pretend." This border pattern represents a "pretend window." Traditionally, the men's community house and public meeting place (*qasgiq*) and the sod homes had one window that was located on the ceiling in the center of the home. It was made of dried seal gut and was stretched over a wooden frame.

Elirqaaq—shape cut to be used in a pattern (use a *elirqun* to make a *elirqaaq*).

Elirqumalriit tumartarkat—shapes, a group to be sewn together.

Elirqun—shape used as a template to cut out other shapes (shape used as a tool to cut something out).

Ikamram—the base word is *ikamraq*, which means "a sled." This sled was traditionally made of wood, was pulled by dogs, and carried heavy loads. The word *ikamra ˉm* means "the sled's," which would be followed with a description.

Ingriruaq—the base word is *ingriq*, which means "a mountain" (singular), and the ending *–uaq* means "pretend." This border pattern represents a "pretend mountain." The Yup'ik people live in many areas of Alaska and mountains surround some of those areas.

Ingriruat—the base word is *ingriq*, which means "a mountain" (singular), and the ending *–uaq* means "pretend." This border pattern represents "pretend mountains" (plural) if it ends with the letter "*t*."

Iluvaktuq—the base word is *ilu*, which is the intestinal tract. This is a legendary Yup'ik man's name, which literally means that he had a big appetite.

Kangirak—two corners.

Kangirenqellria—square, standard orientation (one with perfect corners); also *yaassiik* (square or box, from the Russian *yashchik*); *yaassiigenqellria* (one that is a perfect box).

Katngisnguaq—tip of the middle finger.

Keggutnguat—the base word is *keggute–,* which means "a tooth," and the ending *–nguat* means "pretend." This pattern represents a "pretend tooth." This may represent many different animals and fish that are found in the natural environment of the Yup'ik people, such as the bear, wolf, wolverine, and different species of fish.

Kegluneq—wolf.

Nunurat—the smaller rectangular piece.

Paluqtaq—beaver.

Pitegcautnguaq—pretend arrow.

Qemirrlugun—the larger rectangular piece with tassels and family symbols.

Qulitaq—the part of the parka which hangs from the shoulder and includes family symbols.

Takuralria ciligcimalria—rhombus (something stretched and tilted).

Terikaniaq—wolverine.

Tumaqcat—pieces; a set that can be copied to make a whole pattern.

Tumaqluki—putting the pieces together (process).

Tumarciq—putting pieces together to make patterns.

Tumartat—pieces put together to make a whole (product).

Tumellri—the base word *tuma* literally means "path." *Tumellri* means "the path that is made."

Tungliqurluteng ayuqellriit—pattern with repeating shapes.

Tusruteq—shoulder symbol on a man's parka.

Urluvruaq—pretend bow.

Yaassiik—box.

Yaassiiguaq—this word refers to a square. The base word is *yaassik*, which means "a box," and the ending *–uaq* means "pretend" in singular form. This repeating border pattern reveals a "pretend box." Traditionally, the Yup'ik people valued boxes that were made of wood, as they were rare to come by. Those who lived out in the tundra or along the coast, where wood was scarce, valued them especially.

Yaassiiguat—this word refers to a square. The base word is *yaassik*, which means "a box," and the ending *–guat* means "pretend" (plus two or more). This repeating border pattern reveals "pretend boxes." Traditionally, the Yup'ik people valued boxes that were made of wood, as they were rare to come by. Those who lived out in the tundra or along the coast, where wood was scarce, valued them especially.

Yup'ik—the base word is *Yug*, which means "a person, human being." *Pik* means "the real thing." Yup'ik literally means "a real person." Yup'ik are a subgroup under the branch of the Eskimo. The Yup'ik Eskimos live in the Southwestern part of Alaska. The Eskimo language that they speak is called Yup'ik Eskimo, which distinguishes itself from other Eskimo languages.

Yup'ik Shape Names

Circle—*akagenqellria* or *uivenqellria* (one that goes around easily, one that rotates perfectly).

Line, slanted—*ciligtellria*.

Line, straight—*nalqilria*.

Lines, two slanted (balanced symmetrically)—*ciligtellriik*.

Oval—*uivlugtellria* (one that's something like a circle but doesn't rotate properly).

Parallelogram—*nalqilriik ituklutek* (two that are put along side each other and properly aligned or parallel).

Rectangle (with long side flat)—*taksurenqellria yaassiik* (box that is long).

Rectangle (with short side flat)—*naparenqellria yaassiik* (box that is straight up).

Rhombus—*takuralria ciligcimalria* (something stretched and tilted; same as tilted square).

Right isosceles triangle—*ciligcimalria yaassiigenqellria* (cut from a square at an angle).

Square, standard orientation—*kangirenqellria* (one with perfect corners); also *yaassiik* (square or box, from the Russian *yashchik*); *yaassiigenqellria* (one that is a perfect box).

Square, tilted—*ciligcimalria yaassiigenqellria* (a square turned at an angle; same as rhombus).

Triangle—*pingayunek kangiralek* (one with three corners)

Master Materials List

Teacher Provides

Adding machine tape or some other continuous strip
  of paper

Butcher paper: white and other color

Construction paper: black, white, and an additional
  color

Crayons

Glue sticks or glue

Markers

Math notebooks for students

Overhead projector

Parka or doll wearing parka (optional)

Pencils

Scissors

Envelopes: two for each student, one for collecting
  scraps and for one holding their parka pattern
  pieces (10 inches by 13 inches)

Transparencies: blank

Yarn: red, black, and white

Samples to be Provided by Teacher

Bookmark for Activity 3

Calfskin, if available see page 119 for an example of
  simulated (paper) calfskin for Exploration A

Large shapes in construction paper: square, triangle,
  rectangle, circle, rhombus, parallelogram for
  Activity 1

Paper Ruff for Exploration C

Precut pattern pieces (*tumaqcat*), different shapes
  and sizes for Activity 1

Sample tassels (see Explorations A, B)

Package Includes

CD-ROM, Yup'ik Glossary

DVD, *Tumartat*: Putting the Pieces Together to
  Make a Whole

DVD Lessons:

1   Folding a Perfect Square, demonstrated by
     Anecia Toyukak, Manokotak, Alaska

2   Making a Strip of Squares, demonstrated by
     Anuska Nanalook, Manokotak, Alaska

3   Making Squares, Step by Step Demonstra-
     tion

4   Square to Circle, demonstrated by Dora
     Andrew-Ihrke, Anchorage, Alaska

5.1 Rectangle to Rhombus, demonstrated by
     Mary Beans, St Mary's, Alaska

5.2 Rectangle to Rhombus, Step by Step

5.3 Rectangle to Rhombus, demonstrated by
     Mary Beans, St Mary's Alaska

6   Rectangle to Fancy Rhombus, Step by Step,
     demonstrated by Winifred Beans, St Mary's.
     Alaska

7   Square to Parallelogram, demonstrated by
     Anecia Toyukak, Manokotak, Alaska

Posters

Yup'ik Border Patterns (*Tumaqcat wall'u Kepuqcat*)

Yup'ik Parka Posters:

  Parka with Pretend Boxes (*Yaassiiguat*)

  Parka with Pretend Boxes on Top of Each Other
  and Connected (*Qulliqellriit yaassiiguat*)

  Parka with Pretend Braids (*Taquruat*)

  Parka with Pretend Mountains with Reflections
  (*Ingriruat tarenrarluteng*)

  Parka with Pretend Teeth or Mountains (*Keggutnguat* or *Ingriruat*)

  Parka with Pretend Windows (*Egaleruat*)

Blackline Masters for Transparencies

Annie Blue's Parka, Front

Annie Blue's Parka, Back

More Squares—Creating Basic Units (optional)
Shapes of Properties Chart (optional)
What's Missing? Part 1
What's Missing? Part 2
What's Next? Part 1
What's Next? Part 2
Yup'ik Border Patterns (*Tumaqcat wall' u Kepuqcat*)
Yup'ik Parkas:
    Parka with Pretend Boxes (*Yaassiiguat*)
    Parka with Pretend Boxes on Top of Each Other
    and Connected (*Qulliqellriit yaassiiguat*)
    Parka with Pretend Braids (*Taquruat*)
    Parka with Pretend Mountains with Reflections
    (*Ingriruat tarenrarluteng*)
    Parka with Pretend Teeth or Mountains (*Keg-gutnguat* or *Ingriruat*)
    Parka with Pretend Windows (*Egaleruat*)

Blackline Masters for Worksheets

Measuring with a Bookmark
More Squares—Creating Basic Units
Parka Ruff (*Asguruaq*)
Recording Paper
Shape Properties Chart
Shapes for Sorting
What's Missing? Part 1
What's Missing? Part 2
What's Next? Part 1
What's Next? Part 2

Suggested to Accompany the Module

Iluvaktuq storybook for grade 2, available from
    Detselig Enterprises Ltd., 210-1220 Kensington
    Rd. NW, Calgary, AB T2N 3P5, Canada.
    Phone: (403) 283-0900, Fax: (403) 283-6947
    E-mail: temeron@telusplanet.net
    www.temerondetselig.com

References

Alaska Native Heritage Center. 2006. *Ilairutaq -Yup'ik woman's fancy parka* 2000 [cited December 29 2006]. Available from http://www.alaskanative.net/192.asp.

Alaska Native Knowledge Network. 2006. *Alaska standards for culturally responsive schools.* University of Alaska Fairbanks 1998 [cited December 28 2006]. Available from http://www.ankn.uaf.edu/publications/#standards.

Collins, Allan, John Seely Brown, and Susan E. Newman. 1989. Cognitive apprenticeship: teaching the craft of reading, writing and mathematics. In *Knowing, learning and instruction: Essays in honor of Robert Glaser,* edited by R. Glaser and L. B. Resnick. Hillsdale, NJ: Lawrence Erlbaum Associates.

Harris, Pamela. 1991. *Mathematics in a cultural context: Aboriginal perspectives on space, time, and money.* Geelong, Victoria: Deakin University.

James, Glenn, Robert C. James, and Armen Albert Alchian. 1968. *Mathematics dictionary.* 3d ed. Princeton, NJ: Van Nostrand Reinhold.

Lee, C. D. 1995. A culturally based cognitive apprenticeship: Teaching African American high school students skills in literary interpretation. *Reading Research Quarterly* 30:606-630.

Lipka, Jerry, Nancy Sharp, Mary Brenner, Evelyn Yanez, and Ferdinand Sharp. 2005. The relevance of culturally based curriculum and instructions: The case of Nancy Sharp. *Journal of American Indian Education* 44 (3):30-54.

Lipka, Jerry, and Evelyn Yanez. 1998. Identifying and understanding cultural differences: Toward culturally based pedagogy. In *Transforming the culture of schools: Yup'ik Eskimo examples.* Mahwah, NJ: Lawrence Erlbaum and Associates.

National Council of Teachers of Mathematics. 2000. *Curriculum and evaluation standards.* Reston, VA: National Council of Teachers of Mathematics.

Otto, Whitney. 1991. *How to make an American quilt.* New York: Villard Books.

Rogoff, Barbara. 1990. *Apprenticeship in thinking. Cognitive development in social context.* New York, NY: Oxford University Press, Inc.

Stenmark, Jean Kerr. 1989. *Assessment alternatives in mathematics*: EQUALS, Lawrence Hall of Science, University of California, Berkeley.

Washburn, Dorothy Koster, and Donald W. Crowe. 1988. *Symmetries of culture: theory and practice of plane pattern analysis.* Seattle: University of Washington Press.

Internet Resources

http://www.linkslearning.org/Kids/1_Math/2_Illustrated_Lessons/2_Estimation_of_Length/index.html
This is an excellent source for estimating length, place value, symmetry, patterns, weight and capacity, and tangrams.

Patterns and

Putting the Pieces Together to Make a Whole (*Tumartat*)

1

In *Tumartat*: Putting the Pieces Together to Make a Whole, students identify, describe, and understand geometrical relationships. The idea of conservation of area develops as they create shapes, basic units made from shapes, and repeating patterns made by repeating the basic units. Students start with a square, decompose the square into different shapes, and recompose those shapes into other shapes or basic units that are then repeated to make a pattern. This is called *tumartat,* "putting the pieces together to make a whole."

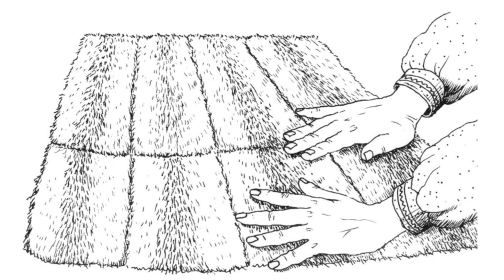

Activity 1
Discovering a Square

Fig. 1.1: Pretend boxes border pattern

Keeping in mind the continuous border pattern on a squirrel parka, the Yup'ik elder may choose a square as the basic unit of measure for a particular project. Some seamstresses will imagine the finished product, the parka, estimating the width of the pattern and the circumference of the parka's lower edge, by mentally partitioning the circumference to visualize a square. She then cuts out this square, and uses it as a unit of measure to make the pieces for a pleasing parka design.

Throughout this module, your class will be learning the whole process of making a repeating pattern, the border used to decorate a parka, starting with the first piece, the basic unit—the square. Students will be forced to use problem solving techniques.

Fig. 1.2: Examples of completed student work: paper parkas and pattern designs

The making of the first square sets the pattern of learning for the entire module. The pattern of action, proof, and refinement is set by the pedagogy, which includes expert-apprentice modeling and joint productive activity. In each of these, the teacher makes a square as the students watch, before designing and creating their own original work. Students also analyze their work, using the mathematical concepts of conjecture and proof. Just like the Yup'ik elder seamstress, your students will become creators and designers of patterns throughout this module. They will begin this activity by focusing on a square, expanding their knowledge of geometry while creating a square unit, folding on lines of symmetry, and proving that a unit is a square.

More specifically, students will problem solve by attempting to cut a square from an irregularly shaped piece of paper without using any standard measuring tools. Students are encouraged to prove their unit is a square by folding it on the lines of symmetry (the diagonals and the horizontal and vertical axes), and by identifying the properties of a square. Your students will communicate physical proofs, verbally, and in writing to others. They will also explore other methods of cutting out squares.

Extensive time is devoted to this activity because the concepts of shape, symmetry, congruence, properties, and proof are introduced. Symmetry and congruence become mathematical "tools" for students as they create other shapes from the square. Through this process they explore and discover properties of rectangles, parallelograms, and triangles. An understanding of the properties of geometrical shapes develops as students observe, practice, and perfect their shapes in the first two activities of the module.

Because of the important relationship between math concepts and having the vocabulary to express those concepts throughout this module, students will be engaged in a variety of literacy activities. Begin reading the story of Iluvaktuq in the next day or two. This module supports literacy by building students' vocabularies, and this occurs in a variety of ways, such as through their use of pantomime to describe geometrical properties, and through journaling. Math notebooks are used throughout the module for students to express their understanding of mathematical concepts and processes. You may choose to have them write about the Yup'ik culture, their understanding of the activity, the math involved, or where they see shapes and patterns in their environment. You may also want to use a large flip chart to record a daily notebook entry. This is useful for modeling, for review, or to help a student who has been absent catch up quickly.

At the end of this activity, there is a series of parkas and patterns. During the course of the first few activities, introduce these to your students by showing them the posters of Yup'ik parkas with various border patterns. Display the posters in the classroom.

Goals

- To use observation to learn a new skill: making a square
- To visually conceptualize a particular size of square
- To describe the properties of a square and to compare squares with other shapes
- To explore and identify a square's lines of symmetry
- To make and prove simple mathematical conjectures about squares

Materials

- Butcher paper
- DVD, *Tumartat: Putting the Pieces Together to Make a Whole*
- Irregularly shaped pieces of white or black paper, approximately 9 inches by 9 inches
- Large shapes: square, triangle, rectangle, circle, rhombus, parallelogram, etc.
- Math notebooks
- Poster and Transparency, Parka with Pretend Boxes Pattern
- Poster and Transparency, Parka with Pretend Boxes on Top of Each Other and Connected Pattern
- Poster and Transparency, Parka with Pretend Braids Pattern
- Poster and Transparency, Parka with Pretend Mountains Pattern
- Poster and Transparency, Parka with Pretend Mountains with Reflections Pattern
- Poster and Transparency, Parka with Pretend Teeth Pattern
- Poster and Transparency, Parka with Pretend Windows Pattern
- Poster and Transparency, Yup'ik Border Patterns (*Tumaqcat wall' u Kepuqcat*)
- Precut 3 inches by 6 inches strips of construction paper in black and white, one per student
- Scissors
- Two envelopes 10 inches by 13 inches per student (one for collecting scraps and one for holding their parka pattern pieces)
- Worksheet, Recording Paper

Duration

Two or three class periods.

Vocabulary

Angle—a geometric figure formed when two lines, rays, or line segments meet at a point. The meeting point is called the vertex of the angle. An angle is measured in degrees of rotation between the two lines, rays, or line segments.

Center—a point that is equidistant from all *points* in a circle; a point that is equidistant from all *sides* of a regular polygon.

Congruence—the property of two shapes that are congruent.

Congruent—geometric figures (or parts of figures) that are the same shape and size. Two shapes are congruent if one shape can be slid, flipped, and/or rotated so that the shape fits exactly on top of the other one. Parts of a shape—for example, sides or angles—may also be congruent.

Conjecture—a statement about a mathematical fact, relationship, or generalization that is based on careful observation or experimentation but which has not been proven. (See Proof)

Diagonal—a line segment opposite vertices of any quadrilateral.

Line of symmetry—a line that is a property of a geometric figure (a shape, design, or pattern); it divides the figure into two equal parts, such that when the figure is reflected about that line, the result is identical to the starting figure. For example, a square has four lines of symmetry: one vertical, one horizontal, and two diagonal lines through the center. An informal test for a line of symmetry in a two-dimensional shape is to fold the shape along a line through its center. If both sides match exactly after folding, the line is a line of symmetry.

Mirror symmetry—a property of a geometric figure with one or more lines of symmetry. If you place a mirror along a line of symmetry, the visual effect is that the half of the object and its reflection look exactly like the complete object.

Pattern—a design that consists of a basic repeating unit repeated over and over again; a pattern may be extended in one direction (linear or frieze pattern), two directions (two-dimensional or "wallpaper" pattern), or three directions (crystal pattern).

Proof—a mathematical argument, based on logical reasoning, that demonstrates that a particular fact or relationship is true. (See Conjecture)

Properties—the attributes of a geometric shape (sides, angles, symmetries and their relationships) that define a particular shape as a unique shape. For example, the basic properties of a square are that it has four equal sides and four equal angles. From these stem additional properties: its angles all equal 90 degrees, it has four lines of symmetry, and it is rotationally symmetrical when rotated 90 degrees about its center.

Rectangle—a quadrilateral with four equal angles, all equal to 90 degrees. Its opposite sides are parallel and equal to each other. Alternatively, a rectangle is a parallelogram with all angles equal.

Rotational symmetry—the quality of a geometric figure (shape, design, or pattern) such that when the figure is rotated about a given point, through a particular angle, the result is identical to the original shape. For example, when a square is rotated about its center through exactly 90 degrees, the result is identical to the square before it was rotated.

Shape—form or outline.

Square—a regular quadrilateral. All sides have the same length, and all the
angles are right angles. Alternatively, a square is a rectangle with all sides
the same length.

Symmetry—a quality of a shape such that the shape does not change when
transformed by a rigid transformation. There are three types of symmetry:
line symmetry (or mirror symmetry), rotational symmetry (or point symmetry), and translational symmetry.

Translational symmetry—a property of a geometric figure such that the figure
is repeated moving along a line in any direction.

Unit of measure—a scale used to record measurements of length, area, temperature,
etc.

Vertical line—a line perpendicular to the ground, or the bottom of a figure, or
a piece of paper. Vertical and horizontal lines meet at right angles.

Preparation

If possible, obtain a parka for the students to look at, feel, and try on. Show the
students examples of the parka borders. View the DVD *Tumartat*: *Putting the
Pieces Together to Make a Whole*. It shows how Anuska Nanalook, an elder from
Manokotak, Alaska, folds a square from irregular material. It also shows her making a square by folding the corner of a rectangle. Preview the lessons pertaining
to a square and select lessons and clips to be used throughout the module.

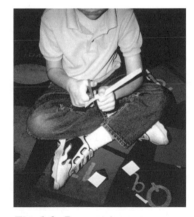

Fig. 1.3: Boy cutting a square

Tear irregularly shaped pieces of paper, black or white, (a standard piece of
paper with all straight edges torn off works well) for students to use for cutting
squares. Prepare a space for recording student responses. You or the students may
write their conjectures on the recording paper or on the blackboard. Prepare a
space to display yours' and the students' squares. Make large samples of shapes:
square, triangle, rectangle, circle, rhombus, etc. Make some non-examples of a
square to display with student work. Display the Yup'ik Border Patterns poster,
and Parka posters around the room. Model keeping a notebook as you work
through the module, recording your conjectures, discoveries, and any pleasing
patterns you see or design. (Begin work on the parka in Explorations A–D)

Practice making a square from an irregular shaped piece of paper—described
in Part 1 Instruction 6—so that you can model this process for your students.

Teacher
Note

Record student responses
because this information
assesses their understanding of shapes in general and
the properties of a square in
particular. They may recognize that a square has four
sides and that all four sides
are equal. This is a good
starting point—but it is not
enough to define a square.
As they continue to work
with squares they should
recognize that the four
angles are also equal.

Teacher
Note

As you cut your square,
share cultural information
regarding conservation of
materials. Some students
will cut their first square out
of the middle of the paper
and then will not have a big
enough piece from which
to cut the second square.
Have extra torn pieces of
paper available. Have the
students save the scrap
paper to compare their
use of materials with each
other.

Part 1: Making a Square from Irregularly Shaped Paper

Instructions

1. Explain that for the next few weeks your class will be learning about the Yup'ik Eskimo culture and the process of making a repeating pattern (show one), the border used to decorate a parka. Students will study Yup'ik Eskimo traditional patterns, and how people make their own designs; stress that students will make their own Yup'ik pattern pieces (*tumaqcat*) and create designs and patterns.

2. Display posters, point out the parka borders, and ask the students what shapes and patterns they see. The students may name a shape or point to a shape.

3. Have prepared shapes available and have the students identify which shapes are squares. Ask your students, "What makes them squares?" Record students' responses to use later in the lesson.

4. Hold up a rectangle and a square, ask the students how are they different and how are they same. Record responses.

5. Explain the purpose for cutting a square from an irregular piece of paper. We are using irregular paper because when Yup'ik people make patterns they usually make them from irregular material. They make shapes with as little waste as possible. Tell the students that they will be cutting two squares, one now and one later, so they must use their paper wisely. This will help them decide how big to make their squares.

6. Model cutting a square from an irregular piece of paper (see Figure 1.4) and/or show the DVD *Tumartat*: *Putting the Pieces Together to Make a Whole* as a way to model this process. As you do this explain or point out how you know it is a square. **Teacher Note:** (1) Starting with your irregularly shaped piece of paper, make a straight fold near one edge. (2) Fold a second edge at right angles to the first by folding the first edge back along itself. (3) Open the folds and cut along them to form a piece of paper with one square corner. (4) Now, make a fold parallel to the shorter edge so that the folded part of the long edge lines up with itself and cut carefully along the line where the edge meets the paper. You now have two right angles and two parallel lines. (5) Now fold through one corner so that the top and side edges line up and cut carefully along the line where the edge meets the paper. You now have a shape that is very close to a square. (6) Unfold and refold along the opposite diagonal. Trim your square by carefully folding along all four lines of symmetry and cutting off edges so that the sides match.

7. Joint Activity. Hand out small irregular pieces of butcher paper and scissors. Without the use of any measuring device, have the students visualize an approximately 3- inch square shape and have them cut one square that size. Begin cutting your own square. Students can follow along, and when they think they know how to do it, they may try to continue on their own.

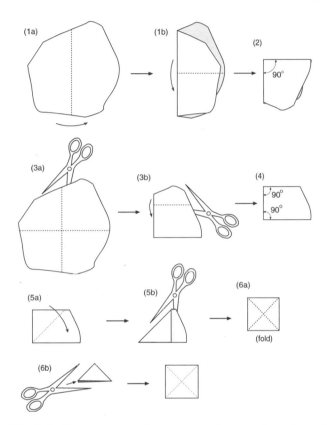

Fig. 1.4: One way to make a square from an irregular piece of paper

8. Introduce the term *line of symmetry* after you have made your square. Explain that if you can fold a shape in half and both sides match exactly, then it has a line of symmetry. Ask students to think about how many different lines of symmetry they can find when they make their own squares.

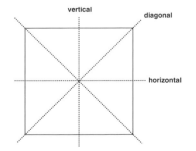

Fig. 1.5: Square with lines of symmetry

Fig. 1.6: Joint activity: Nancy Sharp and her students make squares

Teacher Note

A reasonable prediction that is not yet proven is called a conjecture. When students have an idea in mind, they should fold the square to verify and prove or disprove their conjecture. If the two sides are not the same, students make another conjecture on where they can fold the square so both sides are the same, then fold the square again to find a line of symmetry.

9. Peer sharing. Ask the students, "How do you know your shape is a square?" Have them *prove or disprove* whether their shape is a square to a partner. Allow two to three minutes for sharing. If necessary, model peer sharing and proving a shape is a square.

10. Ask for volunteers to share their method of proving a shape is a square. Repeat and record their ideas. Write a list of properties of a square on butcher paper. Add to this list as students gain new insights. Add other shapes to this list. Hand out Recording Paper worksheet. **Teacher Note:** Students are starting to think of the properties of a square. Refer to properties of shapes in the introduction for more information.

11. **Challenge.** How many ways can you fold the square in halves so that both halves match each other? Hand out precut squares to each student. Have them predict, record their predictions, and explore.

12. Have the students share their ways of folding a square in half. Were their predictions correct? Have the students write their names on their squares. Collect and display their squares on a piece of butcher paper or the blackboard. (Keep the display for later comparison.)

13. **Math notebooks.** Have students describe and illustrate the properties of a square in their math notebooks.

Depending on your class, this may be a good place to stop for the day. Distribute the storage envelopes and have the students save all the scraps for use in the next part of the lesson. Be sure they write their names on the envelopes. Collect the storage envelopes. Begin the following day with a discussion on properties of a square.

Cultural Note

Some elders mentioned that it was very frustrating when they first started to cut and sew skins. But they also said they just kept trying until they did a good job. When elders were observed teaching younger people to cut a square to use as a template, one person made a 3-inch square, another person made 1-inch square, and still another smaller than 1-inch square. Practice continued until the younger people were satisfied with their squares.

One rural teacher shared a story:

When our oldest son was a baby I tried making him a pair of mukluks [boots]. The beginning stitches were uniform and nice. When I got tired of sewing instead of putting the project down so that I could rest my fingers I kept pushing myself to finish. The stitches became further apart and messy. I showed the one finished mukluk to my mom and asked if they were ok. She looked at them and said, "If you want them to be ok, they're ok. But, when a woman does sewing and it is messy she will always be known as someone who does that type of work. It is your choice though. How do you want to be known? Remember you are known by your work." I took out all the stitches and did it all over again because I did not want to be known as someone who does messy work.

Part 2: Other Methods of Making a Square

We have worked with many Yup'ik elders over the years and many elders have different ways of making squares or other shapes. The different methods have embedded different mathematical relationships. Throughout the module students learn multiple ways of making shapes and multiple ways of investigating the properties of shapes.

Instructions

1. Pantomime. Review properties of a square. Ask the students to imagine that they will be explaining the properties of a square without speaking. Have one student at a time demonstrate a property. (Properties might include: all four sides equal; all four angles equal; line of symmetry shown by folding through center parallel to an edge; line of symmetry shown by folding along diagonal.) Have students determine the property.

2. Remind the students that during the next few weeks they will be making a lot of squares to use in their designs and patterns. Explain to the students that they will explore other ways to make squares quickly to use in decorating their borders.

3. Show the DVD *Tumartat: Putting the Pieces Together to Make a Whole.* It shows how Anuska Nanalook makes a square by folding one side of a

rectangle. Hand out a 3 inches by 6 inches strip of paper. Have the students observe and make a square following her method.

4. Have the students explore a different method for making a square from a nonsquare shape. Distribute scissors; two strips of construction paper cut to 3 inches by 6 inches, one white and one black; and the envelopes, one for storing pattern pieces and the other for waste to each student.

5. Ask the students how they can use the two strips of construction paper to make squares.

6. Allow time for students to explore and make squares.

7. Call on volunteers to show and explain their methods. Have them demonstrate to the class.

Teacher Note

Students' work will vary depending on many things: developmental stage, attitude, interest, and skill, to name a few. Their finished squares are self-evaluated and accepted or rejected according to their comparison to your sample, their first sample, and their personal idea or mental image of a

8. Explain that Yup'ik elders try to make their squares as close to perfect as possible so that when they use their shapes to make patterns, the shapes will line up correctly without leaving gaps in their patterns. Ask students to compare the squares they made yesterday with the ones they made today. Which one do they think is closer to a "perfect" square? How can they tell?

9. Demonstrate how a square and a rectangle differ. Cut two squares at the same time. Now rotate them atop each other. The sides and corners should

Teacher Note

If the students did not discover the following methods, model while the students observe and imitate. 1) Compare the black and white strips to be sure they are the same width. Cross the black and the white strips at right angles so that the long edge of one paper is flush with the short edge of the other. Cut the black paper along the opposite edge of the white paper, forming a black square. Align the papers

match up no matter which way you turn them. Continue to rotate the top square until the two squares match again. Lead children to discover that there are four different positions in which the top square matches the bottom square. This is rotational symmetry. Now cut out two congruent rectangles. Ask the students what will happen if we rotate the rectangle as we did the square? (There are only two positions where the rectangles match.) Demonstrate and discuss.

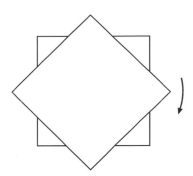

Fig. 1.7: Rotational symmetry

10. **Challenge.** How many lines of symmetry does a rectangle have?

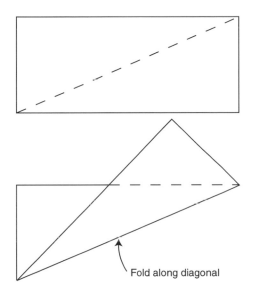

Fold along diagonal

Fig. 1.8: Diagonals of a rectangle are not lines of symmetry

11. Make a chart of shape properties on butcher paper:

Properties of a square	Properties of a rectangle
• Four equal sides • Four square angles (or right angles) • Four lines of symmetry (through center parallel to edges and along diagonals)	• Opposite sides equal • Four square angles (or right angles) • Two lines of symmetry (through center parallel to edges)

Fig. 1.9: Chart of shape properties

12. **Math notebooks.** Have the students share their processes for making and verifying squares. Ask them to explain how they can tell whether a shape is square or not.

Math and Cultural Note: Three Ways to Make a Square from a Rectangle

The rectangle and square share the properties that all four angles are equal to 90 degrees and that opposite sides are equal and parallel.

We asked Anuska Nanalook, an elder from Manokotak, Alaska, how she makes a square. The first method of making a square is paraphrased below:

> *One method she uses is to fold the square corner of a piece of paper on a diagonal and cut along the sides of the triangle. When the corner is then folded open, a square shape is produced. (Figure 1.10) The Sears catalog was used before paper was available, and before that the straight grain of the material in sugar or flour sacks was used. (Translation)*

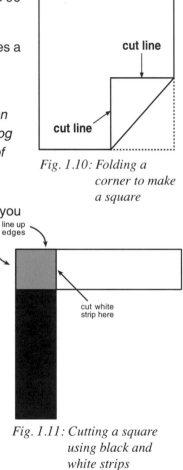

Fig. 1.10: Folding a corner to make a square

Using the second method (Figure 1.11) for cutting a square from a rectangle, you use two rectangles with the same width. When one is placed on top of the other as shown, the space where they overlap forms a square whose length is the width of the original rectangle.

The third method (Figure 1.12) is another way of cutting a rectangle to create a square whose length is the width of the original rectangle. When you fold the corner of the rectangle, you are in effect, using the shorter side of the rectangle as a ruler to measure off a new length along the longer side. When you cut along the line where the folded edge meets the rectangle, you create a new shape with four 90 degree angles and equal sides. You have thereby cut a square out of a rectangle.

Fig. 1.11: Cutting a square using black and white strips

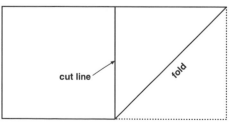

Fig. 1.12: Rectangle folded to make a square

Assist students with their first few notebook entries by modeling. Ask students to share their ideas with you to help you write your own notebook entry. Using the overhead, butcher paper, or the board, demonstrate a notebook entry you would consider appropriate. Include drawings to support the writing.

Some students may need to copy your entries at first. Others will want to create their own notebook entries. This will enable all children to be able to share the math ideas from their lessons with fellow students, teachers, and parents.

13. Distribute the storage envelopes and have the students save all the scraps for use later in the activities so they will not be wasted. Collect the storage envelopes.

Assessment

Assess the first and second squares posted for display. Collect the math notebooks and check for understanding of the distinguishing characteristics of a square, symmetry of a square, lines of symmetry, and conservation of materials. Ask students to describe the similarities and differences between a square and a rectangle. Students should be able to:

- say that both have four sides, that opposite sides are equal and that they have the same angles (or corners).
- say that all four sides of a square are equal, and that this is not true for a rectangle.
- understand that a rectangle is like a square that has been stretched in one direction—or conversely, a square is like a rectangle that has been shrunk in one direction.
- demonstrate by folding that a square has four lines of symmetry—through the middles of the sides and along the diagonals. A rectangle, on the other hand, has only two lines of symmetry—through the midpoints of the sides.

Cultural Note: Dora Andrew-Ihrke Makes a

Here is another way to make a square. Dora Andrew-Ihrke, a retired teacher and bilingual coordinator from Dillingham City Schools (Dillingham, Alaska), has learned these techniques from her work with elders. Dora is a consultant to the MCC project.

1. Use any straight edge to draw a line across a piece of paper. (Dora's mother used the edge cut from a box of pilot crackers).

   Then, cut along the line.

2. Measure and mark two knuckle lengths perpendicular to the cut.

3. Make a fold parallel to the cut edge, so that the cut line meets the second mark. Draw a line where the cut edge meets the paper.

4. Cut along the line to make a strip, and open up the fold.

5. Measure one knuckle from the center.

6. Fold the strip across itself to form a right angle. Draw a line across the strip. Then cut along the line.

7. Fold with dot at the centerpoint. Draw a line across the strip again and cut along the line, unfold to reveal the square.

8. Fold your rough square so that the opposite corners match (diagonal fold), then fold along horizontal and vertical lines of symmetry. Trim off any irregularities to make a more exact square.

9. Dora's mother made Dora's father's parka pattern by folding a square three times. Oriented as a diamond, the first fold would break the square into four smaller squares by using the vertical and horizontal lines of symmetry (not diagonals). She then used only one of the smaller squares and folded the corners into the center point, forming four triangles (each 1/8 of the small square) and one smaller square (area totalling 1/2 of the small square). To make the third fold she used only the smaller square and folded it into nine tiny squares in the typical "pretend window" method.

10. Dora's father's pattern was made by alternating the tiny squares, dark and light, in the typical "pretend window" method. The dark tiny squares are each 1/72 of the original square, or 1/18 of each of the smaller squares.

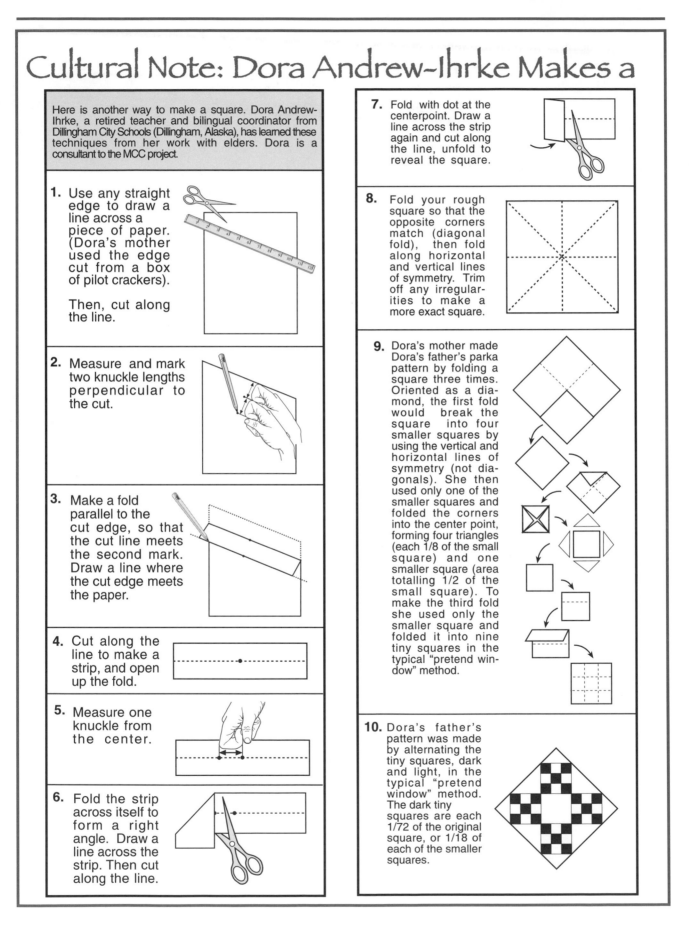

Parka with Pretend Boxes
(*Yaassiiguat*)

Parka with Pretend Boxes on
Top of Each Other and Connected
(*Qulliqellriit yaassiiguat*)

Parka with Pretend Windows
(*Egaleruat*)

Parka with Pretend Teeth or Pretend Mountains
(*Keggutnguat* or *Ingriruat*)

Parka with Pretend Mountains with Reflections
(*Ingriruat tarenrarluteng*)

Parka with Pretend Braids
(*Taquruat*)

MCC

Yup'ik Border Patterns
(Tumaqcat wall'u Kepuqcat)

Pretend boxes (*Yaassiiguat*)

**Pretend boxes on top of each other and connected
(*Qulliqellriit yaassiiguat*)**

Pretend windows (*Egaleruat*)

Pretend teeth or pretend mountains (*Keggutnguat or Ingriruat*)

Pretend mountains with reflections (*Ingriruat tarenrarluteng*)

Pretend braids (*Taquruat*)

Pretend river (*Kuiguaq*)

Pretend sled runners (*Acirnerek/Pirlaa*)

Pretend seashore (*Sen'aruaq*)

Recording Paper Worksheet

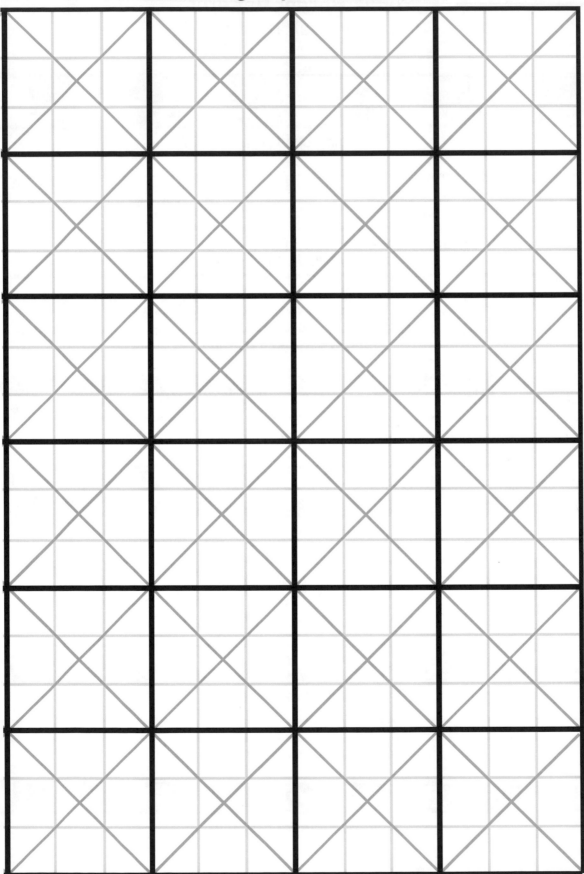

Activity 2
Creating Related Pieces
from the Square

Now that your students feel comfortable making squares, they will use their squares to make other related shapes from the square, providing them with more geometric shapes when designing their patterns. The following sets of activities blend everyday Yup'ik activities such as making parka pattern pieces with constructivist notions of learning math. A distinguishing aspect of this set of activities is that the students, not a commercial company, create and develop their pattern sets. Through this creative and mathematical activity students learn about geometrical relationships. This activity leads them to create other shapes of Yup'ik pattern pieces used for making a border pattern (*tumaqcat*). Later in the module, they may choose to design other shapes to create original patterns for the various projects they will make.

Some Yup'ik seamstresses decide on a design for making a pattern, make the basic square unit, and then make other pieces to complete a border pattern. In this way, the pieces form a whole set that can easily be connected in a linear pattern. This aids in combining the pieces together to form a design that fits together as a whole. If the seamstress chooses a design she has not sewn before, she may draw the pattern to help identify the pieces needed.

Starting with the basic unit of a square, students discover the relationship between the square and the other pieces: triangles, parallelograms, rectangles, and smaller squares. Other shapes are made as students fold and cut the square. Students apply what they learned about symmetry, congruence, and physical proof in the previous activities as they create shapes. This forms a foundation to the math concepts of geometrical relationships.

Students will begin by observing the elder (or teacher) as he or she makes a design with pieces or cuts a square from a sheet of paper. Then the students are challenged to reproduce the intended design.

Goals
* To construct the geometric shapes of the Yup'ik pattern pieces (*tumaqcat*)
* To recognize the geometric relationships among the Yup'ik pattern pieces (*tumaqcat*) and the basic square unit
* To demonstrate conservation of area; the shapes made from the basic square unit have the same area as the square (Example: Two triangles put together have the same area as a square.)

- To recognize, describe, and record the properties of squares, isosceles right triangles, parallelograms, and rectangles
- To identify lines of symmetry and to describe ways of forming new shapes by cutting squares and other shapes along their lines of symmetry
- To explore different ways to form congruent shapes from a square

Materials
- 3-inch black and white construction paper squares, at least five per student
- Butcher paper (optional)
- CD-ROM, *Yup'ik Glossary*
- Math notebooks
- Poster, Parka with Pretend Boxes Pattern
- Poster, Parka with Pretend Boxes on Top of Each Other and Connected Pattern
- Poster, Parka with Pretend Braids Pattern
- Poster, Parka with Pretend Mountains Pattern
- Poster, Parka with Pretend Mountains with Reflections Pattern
- Poster, Parka with Pretend Teeth Pattern
- Poster, Parka with Pretend Windows Pattern
- Poster, Yup'ik Border Patterns (*Tumaqcat wall'u Kepuqcat*)
- Scissors
- Storage envelopes from Activity 1
- Transparency, Shape Properties Chart (optional)
- Worksheet, Recording Paper from Activity 1
- Worksheet, Shape Properties Chart
- Worksheet, Shapes for Sorting

Duration
This activity may take from three to four class periods, depending on the developmental stage of your students. Some students may need more guidance or demonstrations from the teacher than others. Allow students to observe and practice until they recognize the relationship between the different shapes and the square.

Vocabulary
Congruence—the property of two shapes that are congruent.

Congruent—geometric figures (or parts of figures) that are the same shape and size. Two shapes are congruent if one shape can be slid, flipped, and/or rotated so that the shape fits exactly on top of the other one. Parts of a shape—for example, sides or angles—may also be congruent.

Conservation of area—when a shape is divided into two or more parts, all of the parts cover the same total area as the original shape.

Isosceles triangle—a triangle with at least two sides the same length. The angles at the base of an isosceles triangle are also equal.

Line of symmetry—a line that is a property of a geometric figure (a shape, design, or pattern); it divides the figure into two equal parts such that when the figure is reflected about that line, the result is identical to the starting figure. For example, a square has four lines of symmetry: one vertical, one horizontal, and two diagonal lines through the center. An informal test for a line of symmetry in a two-dimensional shape is to fold the shape along a line through its center. If both sides match exactly after folding, the line is a line of symmetry.

Parallelogram—a quadrilateral with both pairs of opposite sides parallel and equal.

Pattern—a design that consists of a basic repeating unit repeated over and over again; a pattern may be extended in one direction (linear or frieze pattern), two directions (two-dimensional or "wallpaper" pattern), or three directions (crystal pattern).

Properties—the attributes of a geometric shape (sides, angles, symmetries and their relationships) that define a particular shape as a unique shape. For example, the basic properties of a square are that it has four equal sides and four equal angles. From these stem additional properties: its angles all equal 90 degrees, it has four lines of symmetry, and it is rotationally symmetrical when rotated 90 degrees about its center.

Quadrilateral—a four-sided polygon.

Rectangle—a quadrilateral with four equal angles, all equal to 90 degrees. Its opposite sides are parallel and equal to each other. Alternatively, a rectangle is a parallelogram with all angles equal.

Shape—form or outline.

Square—a regular quadrilateral. All sides have the same length and all the angles are right angles. Alternatively, a square is a rectangle with all sides the same length.

Triangle—a polygon with three sides.

Tumaqcat—pieces; a set that can be copied to make a whole pattern.

Teacher Note

Explain that now that we can make a square, and we know a little about the properties and symmetry of a square, we will learn to make the other pattern pieces (*tumaqcat)* so we can start using the pieces to make patterns for decorating items for personal use. If the students need help identifying other shapes to make, review the shapes they recognized in the patterns on the posters (squares, large and small; triangles; rectangles; and parallelograms). Explain that the square is the basic unit and that all the other related pieces can be made from the square without creating any wasted material.

Teacher Note

The basic Yup'ik pattern pieces (*tumaqcat*) used in this module begin with a 3-inch square; when folded and cut the square can be made into:

1. Three rectangles, each one-third the area of the square;
2. Nine small squares, each one-ninth the area of the square;
3. Two right isosceles triangles, each one-half the area of the square;
4. One parallelogram (formed with two triangles) with the area equal to the square.

These shapes, when cut out of materials in contrasting colors, form the *tumaqcat,* or basic building blocks from which patterns will be formed later.

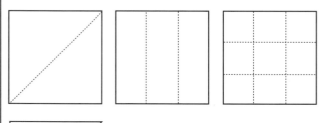

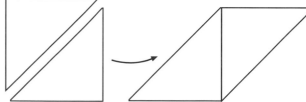

Fig. 2.1: Basic building blocks to make patterns

Many students will struggle while attempting to divide their big square into thirds and ninths when making the rectangles and small squares. Instead, students may prefer to cut their squares into halves, fourths, and even eighths. A set of fractional pieces made into halves, thirds, quarters, eigths, and ninths creates opportunities for explorations into part-whole relationships and fractions.

Fig. 2.2: Diverse set of patterns made in Nancy Sharp's class

Yup'ik educators have demonstrated a relaxed and accepting manner for such developments while teaching. It is very important to note that while elders expect the mature seamstress to develop perfection in her work, this same expectation does not transfer to very young learners. Consequently, perfection while making patterns is not the goal that this module expects from students. Nancy Sharp, a teacher who has piloted this module multiple times and a co-author of this module, encouraged individual creativity rather than having the students reproduce the displayed pattern. Students were challenged to decompose the square and other shapes, then to compose new patterns. The students used problem solving steps and actually used the voids as well as the cut pieces to create pleasing patterns that were unique. The students worked with a black and white color scheme, representing Yup'ik motifs such as mountains, teeth, summer, and winter; each pattern connected to a cultural meaning. Students produced many different designs within the parameters. After observing a videotape of this lesson, Molly Watt, a long-time educator, found that Nancy's students created the most diverse set of patterns she had seen over the years.

Teacher Note

The teaching process we are encouraging is a combination of the Yup'ik way of teaching and "guided" instruction (to make the math explicit). Our understanding is to start with the whole and make the parts, which are then recombined in a pleasing arrangement or pattern to create a new whole. The "whole" in this case, the square, is presented and the students decide what they can do independently and what they need to observe and practice more. Rather than the teacher presenting one step at a time and guiding the students in what they learn, the students attempt to make all the pieces used in *tumaqcat* from the basic unit, the square, learning the relationships of the shapes to the square as they go. Large 3-inch squares are used in this activity because they are easier to fold and cut during exploration of the shapes. Although students may certainly make their own squares, providing precut squares allows more time for math and less time on making squares and developing manual dexterity. While we outline one way of presenting this lesson,

Cultural Note

Yup'ik elders agreed on the word *tumaqcat* for pattern pieces used to make real patterns. The Yup'ik pattern pieces (*tumaqcat*) are based on some of the geometric shapes (in a plane) commonly used to form the repeating patterns on parkas and other decorated objects. The pattern pieces presented in this module are a sample from one region in Alaska, and are not all inclusive. In other regions, different shapes are used as the basic unit, such as the rhombus or rectangle, and related pieces are created to form patterns.

Mary Active, an elder from Togiak, Alaska, explained how she learned to sew,

> Before we started to make dolls we used to storyknife ... drawing people and things that we would make in the future. We didn't do qasperet [dresses], but mukluks [boots], dolls, and later on parkas for dolls. Before I began to sew, I used to watch my mother and then later on she would put the skin side out and make me patch the holes on the parka. When I first started patching the holes, my sewing wasn't that good. They'd be crooked or one side would be too long even though I tried my best. As time went by they got better and better. They were no longer crooked or too long on one side. I learned that that was how it was for all children. When they first start, their stitches are very bad.

Similarly, observing Mayan mothers and children, Barbara Rogoff (1990) noted that children watch a task, such as mak-

Fig. 2.3: A girl storyknifing

Preparation

Read Teacher Notes and Cultural Notes. Gather other materials including the storage envelopes for distribution. Plan to share information with students concerning the Yup'ik way of life. Display the posters in a visible area.

For Part 3, photocopy the Shapes for Sorting worksheet onto construction paper. Cut out the shapes for sorting from the handout. Each pair of students will need one complete set of shapes. Alternatively, distribute the worksheet and let students cut out the shapes.

Part 1: Decomposing a Square

Instructions

1. Show the students some black and some white 3-inch squares you have made. Have a volunteer make a simple pattern with the squares. Ask if there are any other patterns we can make with just black and white squares. Have volunteers share their ideas until they realize there are limited combinations using one shape and two colors.

2. Show the students the Yup'ik Border Patterns poster or transparency. Assist them in identifying the shapes found in the traditional patterns: square, rectangle, triangle, smaller squares, and parallelogram.

3. Ask, "What can we do to have more options for making patterns from our black and white squares?" The students might suggest that they could make other pieces. To help the students, refer them to the poster, Yup'ik Border Patterns.

4. **Challenge.** How can we make varied pattern pieces from the square, using lines of symmetry? Review and model lines of symmetry of a square. Have the students get into small groups or work with a partner. Hand out scissors, two 3-inch squares to each student, and students' storage and scrap envelopes. **Joint activity:** You may model this activity while students are making their pieces. Encourage peer help. Have students make additional shapes to supplement the square. Have the students record the shapes and how they were made from the square in their math notebooks.
    Teacher Note: Students can choose to draw or trace each shape into their math notebooks before going on to create the next shape.

5. Have the students share the shapes that they were able to make and explain how they made them. **Teacher Note:** Pay attention to the students' methods. For example, if the students make smaller right triangles by using all of the lines of symmetry and cut the square accordingly then point this out. Have students check each other's work and ensure that the shapes are formed using the lines of symmetry.

Establish joint ownership of class

6. Show the prepared two congruent right triangles and ask, "How can we make two right triangles from a square?" Have student volunteers show the class on the overhead that two right triangles can form a square. Ask the class, "What is the relationship of the triangles to the square?" Model how two congruent triangles can be made from one square, by cutting along a diagonal line of symmetry, and show that the two triangles have the same area as the square.

7. What other shapes can you make from two right triangles? Challenge the students to make a large triangle or a parallelogram using two triangles. Have students describe their method. **Teacher Note:** Refer to the poster or model again, if students are unable to discover these relationships. Once students have made the shapes, ask them if they can put the triangles back to make a square. This will help them begin to develop the concept of conservation of area: the idea that when geometric shapes are cut apart and the parts are rearranged or combined into new shapes, the total area of the shapes does not change. After exploring, encourage students to tape their new shapes together.

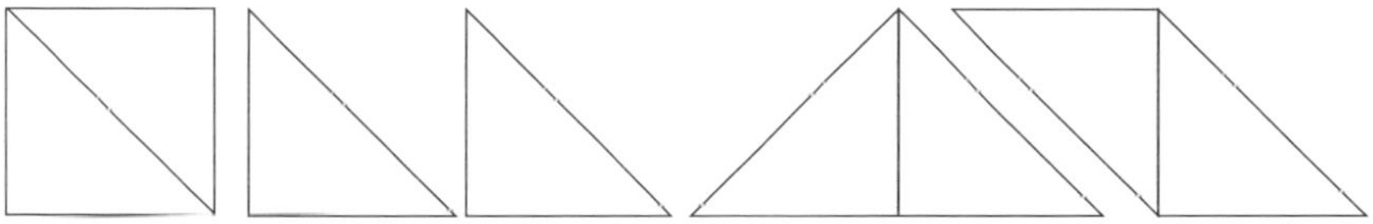

Fig. 2.4: Two triangles, one larger triangle, and a parallelogram all have the same area as the square from which the triangles were cut.

8. Hand out the Shape Properties Chart worksheet and have students (in pairs) complete the chart comparing the properties of the square, rectangle, triangles, and the parallelogram. Encourage students to use and compare the pieces they just made. See Page 70 for the properties of these shapes.

Properties	Original Square	Rectangle	Half-square Triangle	Large Triangle	Parallelogram
How many sides?					
How many equal sides?					
How many angles?					
How many square (90 degree) angles?					
How many lines of symmetry?					

Fig. 2.5: Shape Properties Chart

Teacher Note

Some teachers choose to have the students create a small booklet with each shape glued on a separate page, with the English and Yup'ik names included. The students can use their pattern pieces (*tumaqcat*)

9. Have pairs of student groups share their comparisons. Encourage them to discuss similar/different relationships of the rectangle to the square and the parallelogram to the square. **Teacher Note:** Have the Shape Properties Chart on an overhead transparency or on butcher paper. While students are sharing, list the properties that students come up with on this chart.

10. Once all groups finish sharing, ask the class whether they all agree with the properties listed. If not, ask them to explain why. Also, ask the class for any additional properties that they think could be listed on the chart.

11. **Math notebooks.** Have students include a drawing with the lines of symmetry for each of the four types of shapes. Have them describe the similarities and differences between a square, a rectangle, a triangle, and a parallelogram.

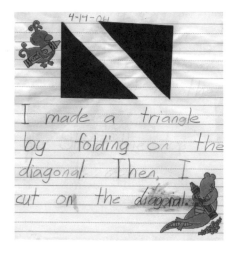

Fig. 2.6: Examples of student work

This may be a good place to stop for the day.

Assessment

Assess how the students are progressing in discovering and making the
other pattern pieces (*tumaqcat*). Review the students' notebooks and Shape
Properties Charts to make sure students can identify the properties of
the shapes that can be made by cutting a square into two right isosceles
triangles. Students should begin to recognize how the properties define and
differentiate the shapes. They should also be grappling with the fact that
when the square is divided and the shapes rearranged, the total area remains
the same. As the students work, walk around and show individuals or small
groups two right isosceles triangles connected to form a square and a square
of the same size. Ask them to point to the shape that is biggest. Then separate
the two triangles and ask them which is biggest now, the two triangles or the
square. Then put the two triangles together by the points so they spread out
like a "butterfly," and repeat your question. Then form a parallelogram and
repeat your question. Are students able to tell you the characteristics shared
by a triangle and a square? How are they the same/different? Ask clarifying
questions to help the students formalize their understanding of the properties
of each shape. As time permits during the next few lessons, continue this
questioning process with rectangles and small squares. These questions will
provide feedback on whether your students can distinguish the properties of
related shapes and understand conservation of area.

Collect the students' notebooks, storage envelopes, and filled-in Shape Properties Charts. Read to understand students' explanations of the shapes, properties
of shapes, lines of symmetry, and the relationship between the square and the
other shapes.

Teacher Note

Note the way students describe the pieces. What are the attributes on which students focus? Do they note the lines of symmetry, even if they do not use the word? What mathematical language do they use? Ask what is the same/different about the shapes. Students are recognizing the properties of the shapes and how they are related to the basic unit, the square. Record their responses for use in Math notebooks later in the lesson. They may have simple answers at first—a triangle is half of a square, it is not the same shape, it only has three sides, it is half the size, etc. Accept and record their answers in a visible place in the room (butcher paper, poster, or blackboard). As the students develop an understanding of the properties and symmetry of the shapes and their answers

Connections can be made to fractions or part/whole

Part 2: Congruent Shapes

Yup'ik parka border patterns usually include several different types of shapes, all derived by dividing a starting square into smaller shapes. Yup'ik design principles include cutting squares along lines of symmetry and lines through midpoints, in order to ensure that the shapes will fit together well and make pleasing patterns. This activity helps students explore different ways of dividing a square into congruent pieces in several different ways. This will help them develop pieces they will use in their patterns for projects in Activities 3 and 5.

Instructions

1. Model constructing smaller rectangles and squares. Explain to students that some of the Yup'ik patterns use thin rectangles and small squares that are made by folding the starting square in thirds. Challenge students to fold one of their squares into three congruent rectangles. Model the folding process for them (see Math Note). Next unfold the square and refold it into thirds in the opposite direction. Ask the students what they can tell about the shapes created by folding. Show them how to test for congruence by cutting out the squares and lining them up, one on top of another, and seeing if they match each other exactly. Explain that these may not be perfect the first time they try. Cutting small shapes with precision takes practice. Explain that they will have many chances to practice cutting out shapes throughout the *Patterns and Parkas* module.

Math Note

Folding a square into thirds is much more challenging than folding it along lines of symmetry, because it is a trial and error process. You have to make a trial fold, and see if all three parts appear to be the same. If so, press the folds together to make them sharp for cutting. If they are not the same, adjust the position of the folds, then check again whether the three parts are congruent before pressing the folds together. Some students may need a good deal of practice before they can fold a 3-inch square into thirds with any degree of accuracy or consistency.

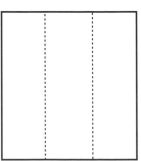

Fig. 2.7: Folding to divide a square into thirds

2. Distribute 3-inch squares and ask students to try to make nine congruent small squares.

3. **Challenge.** Ask students to work with a partner to see whether they can cut a square into congruent shapes in several different ways. Ask the pairs to explore sets of congruent shapes that they can make from the square by folding it in different ways and by cutting along the folds. Suggest that they all start by finding two ways to divide a square into two congruent pieces. Hand out the Recording Paper worksheet and have students draw how they divided the square and record the number of each congruent shape that they made from the square. The most common ways to divide squares into congruent pieces are shown in Figure 2.8.

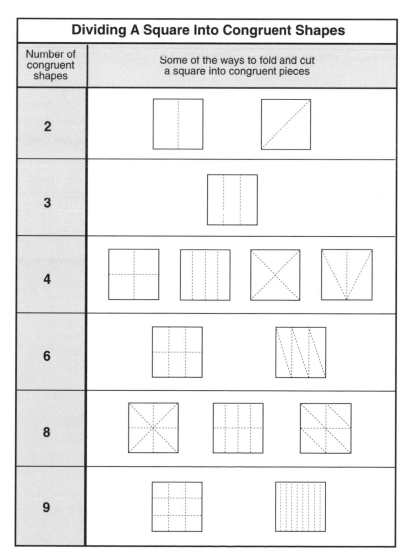

Fig. 2.8: *Dividing a square into congruent shapes*

4. Have students write in their math notebooks. Ask them to pretend to write a letter to a friend telling them one way to divide a square into congruent pieces. Encourage them to use drawings as well as words in their letters.

Extension Activity

5. Rearrange shapes to form new ones. Invite students to create new shapes by rearranging their shapes. Remind students that earlier they used two right triangles to form a square, a larger triangle and a parallelogram.

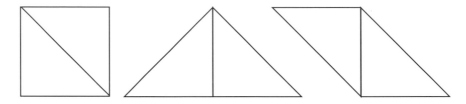

Fig. 2.9: Two right isosceles triangles can form a square, a larger triangle, or a parallelogram

Challenge them to take some of the congruent shapes they just made and rearrange them to form new shapes. As they rearrange their shapes they should make sure that they connect their shapes so that two edges line up with each other. For example, if they are using four triangles, their new shapes might include Design A below, but not Design B (because the edges don't match).

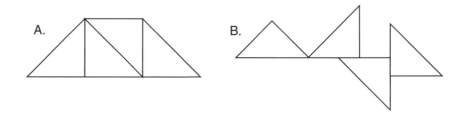

Fig. 2.10: Figure A is considered a valid "new shape" because all the pieces match on at least one edge. In Figure B, the edges don't match

Assessment

As students are working, observe whether they are folding and cutting along lines of symmetry and diagonals. What other strategies do they use to divide the square? Observe whether they are solving problems systematically, that is, solving the simpler ones first, or whether they approach the tasks more randomly. Do they realize that all the pieces cut from one square can be rearranged into new shapes and that the shapes can be recombined to make the original square?

As you read students' notebooks, observe whether they use mathematical language such as "congruent" or "line of symmetry," whether they have their own terms for these concepts, such as "shapes that are the same," and "lines down the middle" or whether these ideas are missing from their descriptions and drawings.

Part 3: Sorting Shapes

By now students have spent a great deal of time folding and cutting shapes, comparing shapes, and describing shape properties. The next part of this activity helps them review and consolidate their knowledge about shape properties as they practice sorting and classifying shapes.

Instructions

1. Model. "I wonder how we can organize these shapes?" Take the Shapes for Sorting worksheet and place it on an overhead projector. Take two different sized squares and say that you decided to put these two shapes together. Ask students to explain why they go together. Ask a student to show another way to categorize two shapes.

2. Hand out the Shapes for Sorting, one to each pair of students and a set of paper plates for each pair. You can substitute other ways of organizing the shapes such as string loops, spaces on the floor, etc.

3. Have students sort these shapes into shapes that go together. This will serve as an assessment of how the students perceive these shapes. Encourage students to work together, and agree on why they put shapes that go together.

4. Have the different pairs of students show the shapes that go together and explain their "rules" for putting the shapes together. Write the students' criteria for placing the shapes together. Pay attention to the attributes that the students perceive as most important for organizing these shapes.

5. Ask students if they can sort all the shapes into exactly two piles. Give students time to do this and ask them what characteristics they used to sort the shapes. Students may sort the shapes into quadrilaterals and triangles; shapes with a line of symmetry and shapes without one; shapes that have at least one right angle, and those that do not. If students can't think of any ways to do this, arrange your shapes on the overhead project into two sets according to one of these rules:

   - Quadrilaterals/triangles
   - Rectangles/not rectangles
   - Shapes with/without a line of symmetry
   - Shapes with two or more lines of symmetry/shapes with one line of symmetry or none
   - Shapes with/without a right angle
   - Fat shapes/thin shapes

Once students have seen one rule, ask them if they could find another rule to divide all the shapes into exactly two piles.

6. Make some charts on a wall with two columns. Write one of the pairings, for example, rectangles/non-rectangles, at the top of each chart. Invite students to come up one at a time and glue or tape one of their shapes on one of the charts. Ask the class if they agree that the shape goes in that column. Once the class has the idea, let all the students come up and place shapes on the charts. When they are finished, review the placements with the whole class. If the class agrees that a shape does not belong, remove it. Keep the charts posted where students can see them.

7. **Math notebooks.** Ask students to choose three different shapes to paste into their notebooks. Ask them to write as many words as they can to describe the properties of each shape.

Assessment

As students are working on sorting activities, observe how comfortable they are with different ways of sorting the same shapes. Can they make up categories of their own for sorting the shapes into two piles? As you read their notebooks, observe which properties they use to describe shapes and which ones they leave out. This can help you plan which concepts to review in future lessons.

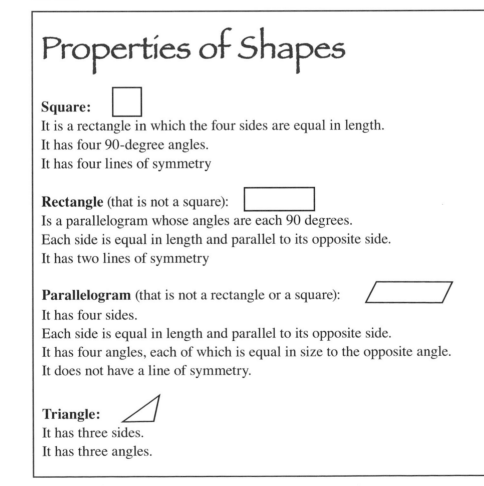

Properties of Shapes

Square:
It is a rectangle in which the four sides are equal in length.
It has four 90-degree angles.
It has four lines of symmetry

Rectangle (that is not a square):
Is a parallelogram whose angles are each 90 degrees.
Each side is equal in length and parallel to its opposite side.
It has two lines of symmetry

Parallelogram (that is not a rectangle or a square):
It has four sides.
Each side is equal in length and parallel to its opposite side.
It has four angles, each of which is equal in size to the opposite angle.
It does not have a line of symmetry.

Triangle:
It has three sides.
It has three angles.

Teacher Note

A square is equal to three rectangles, each ⅓ the area of the square; nine small squares, each ⅑ the area of the square; two triangles, each ½ the area of the square; one parallelogram has the same area as

Shape Properties Chart

Name:_____

Properties	Original Square	Rectangle	Half-square Triangle	Large Triangle	Parallelogram
How many sides?					
How many equal sides?					
How many angles?					
How many square (90 degree) angles?					
How many lines of symmetry?					

Shapes for Sorting

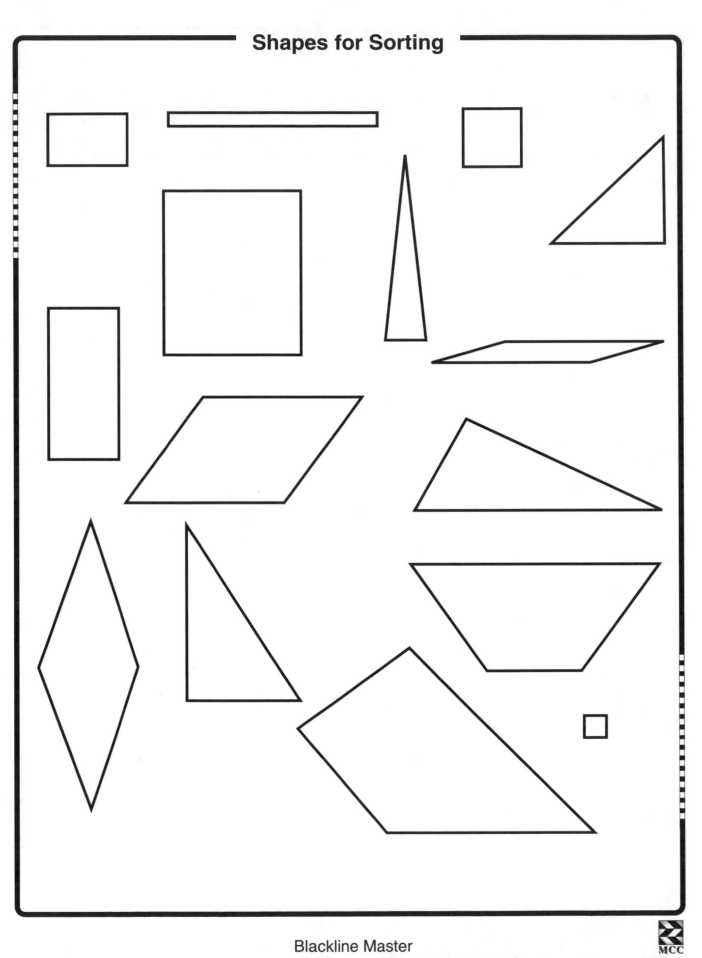

MCC

Activity 3
Repeating Patterns,
Making a Bookmark

Now that your students have their pattern pieces (*tumaqcat*), they can begin to design patterns in order to decorate objects. They will start by creating a bookmark, making it necessary to scale down their original pieces from the previous activities.

After becoming familiar with the pattern pieces (*tumaqcat*) by observing an elder, a beginning seamstress will copy a design she has seen made before, or will create a design of her own. In like fashion, students will learn about the traditional Yup'ik designs: Pretend Box (*Yaassiiguaq*), Pretend Windows (*Egaleruat*), Pretend Teeth (*Keggutnguat*), Pretend Mountains (*Ingriruat*), and Pretend Braids (*Taquruat*). Then your students will have the opportunity to either copy one of these traditional designs or create their own symmetrical, repeating pattern to use for decoration on their bookmark.

When making her border patterns, Anuska Nanalook, an elder in Manokotak, Alaska, begins by choosing a square unit scaled to fit the project, then mentally calculates the number of squares and other pattern pieces (*tumaqcat*) she will need, cuts them all, and has them stacked neatly, prior to beginning her project. Other seamstresses cut one piece at a time, and sew it onto the border pattern. See the accompanying DVD and observe Anuska Nanalook as she plans and creates pattern pieces from irregularly shaped material.

Students will make a bookmark and decorate it with a pattern they design and create using the pattern pieces they construct. Students will notice that the pattern pieces produced from the 3-inch square unit are too large for the 2 ½-inch wide background material used for this project. The teacher models reducing the 3-inch square by folding and cutting on the vertical and horizontal lines of symmetry. The students are then challenged to reduce or scale down the other pattern pieces (*tumaqcat*), the triangle, rectangle, smaller square, and the parallelogram, by folding on the lines of symmetry (*taquruat*) and cutting. The pieces will be based on a square unit measuring 1½ inches for the remainder of the module.

Fig. 3.1: Pretend boxes

One of the designs the students may choose to put on their bookmarks will be the Pretend Box (*yaassiiguaq*). The base word is *yaassiik*, which means "a box," and the ending *-guaq* means "pretend" in singular form. *Yaassiiguat* is the plural form. This border-repeating pattern reveals a pretend box. The pattern is based on the square unit, which you made in Activity 1. Not too long ago, boxes were not a common item in many villages, so a box was highly valued. The value of a box may be the reason the pretend box is so prevalent in border patterns.

Fig. 3.2: Pretend boxes on top of each other and connected

Another design is the pretend windows (*egaleruat*) (Figure 3.4). The base word is *egaleq*, which means "window," and the ending *-uat* means "pretend" in plural form. So, this border pattern means "pretend windows." Traditionally, the men's community house and public meeting place (*qasgiq*) and the sod homes had one window that was located in the center of the roof (see Figure 3.3). It was made of dried seal gut, and was stretched in a wooden frame. Show the students the Yup'ik Border Pattern poster and Parka poster with the pretend windows (*egaleruat*) pattern. Compare this pattern and its name with pretend boxes (*yaassiiguat*). Discuss the patterns and the amount of white and black used to achieve balance.

Fig. 3.3: Sod house with window in center of roof.

Fig. 3.4: Pretend windows

A third traditional pattern is the pretend teeth (*keggutnguat*) (Figure 3.5) or pretend mountains (*ingriruat*). The base word of *keggutnguat* is *keggute*, which means "teeth." The ending, *-guat*, means "pretend" in plural form. Thus, we have "pretend teeth." This may represent many different animals that are found in the natural environment of the Yup'ik people, such as bear, wolf, wolverine, or different species of fish.

Fig. 3.5: Pretend teeth

Fig. 3.6: Pretend mountains with reflections

The base word of *ingriruaq* is *ingriq*, which means "a mountain " and the ending *-uaq* means "pretend." Thus, *ingriruaq* means "pretend mountain." Historically, the Yup'ik people moved several times during the year, relocating to the vicinity of seasonal food sources. During the winter, they retreated to areas protected from the harsh winds. Mountains surrounded many of those areas. Even now, when the Yup'ik spend more time in permanent locations, the mountains rise high in the background of many villages. Thus, *ingriruat* is a reflection of the landscape in which the Yup'ik people live. Since our design will have more than one pretend mountain, we will make *ingriruaq* plural by dropping the "q" and replacing it with a "t," thus *ingriruat*. (Figure 3.6)

Fig. 3.7: View of village and mountains, Manokotak

The final design we will study is pretend braids (*taquruat*) (Figure 3.8). The base word of *taquruat* is *taqur*, which means "to braid." Typically women wear two braids and a man may wear one. When seen from the back, the hood of a parka may have one or two braids as part of the design, making it easier to identify the person ahead of you as a woman or a man.

Fig. 3.8: Pretend braids

Marie Napoka of Tuluksak, Alaska, and the late Mary George of Akiachak, Alaska, first collected the pattern names and shapes noted in this module and on the posters from the elders from Akiachak, Akiak, and Tuluksak, Alaska.

Goals
- To create pattern pieces based on a 1½-inch square, similar to pieces previously made, that were based on a 3-inch square
- To recognize different Yup'ik border patterns
- To create different types of square pattern elements with the *tumaqcat* pieces
- To create a repeating pattern in the form of a bookmark of their own design

Materials
- 1½ inch by 3 inches strips of construction paper, black and white
- 3-inch squares of construction paper, black and white
- 12 inches by 2 ½ inches strips of construction paper in a third color for bookmark backing
- Completed bookmark for demonstration
- Construction paper, optional
- Glue sticks or glue
- Math notebooks
- Poster, Parka with Pretend Boxes Pattern
- Poster, Parka with Pretend Boxes on Top of Each Other and Connected Pattern
- Poster, Parka with Pretend Braids Pattern
- Poster, Parka with Pretend Mountains Pattern
- Poster, Parka with Pretend Mountains with Reflections Pattern
- Poster, Parka with Pretend Teeth Pattern
- Poster, Parka with Pretend Windows Pattern
- Poster, Yup'ik Border Patterns (*Tumaqcat wall'u Kepuqcat*)
- Scissors
- Storage envelopes from previous activities
- Transparency, More Squares—Creating Basic Units, for class demonstration, if needed
- Worksheet, More Squares—Creating Basic Units

Duration
Two or more class periods.

Vocabulary

Orientation—the property of a shape that describes its location in relation to its rotation from a reference line.

Scaling—a nonrigid geometric transformation that shrinks or expands a geometric shape, so that every length in the shape is multiplied by the same ratio, called a "scale factor." Scaling affects only the length of a shape. Its angles are unchanged, and the relative proportions of one length to another are also unchanged.

Preparation

If possible, bring a parka with a border pattern for display. Complete a bookmark to show the class. Be prepared to share your thinking on reducing the size of the square and other related pieces, and how many of each shape you will need. Gather and prepare materials, including the storage envelopes from previous activities with the *tumaqcat* pieces the students made from 3-inch squares. Plan to share information with students concerning the Yup'ik way of life and the Yup'ik traditional patterns.

Part 1: Reducing the Square Unit

Instructions

1. If a parka is available, display it in the room and point out the border pattern. Otherwise display the Parka posters and point out the border patterns.

2. **Discuss.** Show your 3-inch square and the 2 ½ inches by 12 inches backing material for a bookmark. Explain that you want to make a bookmark today using these materials. Ask the students to compare the size of the square in relationship to the backing. What problems do they see and what would they suggest as a solution to the problems? Have students share their ideas with a partner, and ask a few volunteers to share their ideas with the class. (They may recognize that the square is too large to fit on a bookmark and needs to be folded and cut to be reduced to a smaller size.) Remind students of the cultural value of not wasting materials.

3. Challenge students to make four congruent smaller squares from their 3-inch squares. Allow them time to explore doing this.

4. Model with your own project one way of folding and cutting the other shapes to reduce the size so they will fit on the bookmark background material. One way is to scale down the other pattern pieces (*tumaqcat*), originally made from the 3-inch squares, by folding and cutting them into quarters making four new triangles, rectangles, or smaller squares (see Figure 3.9). Another way is to make new pattern pieces from the 1½-inch squares.

Teacher Note

Some students may fold on the diagonal lines of symmetry and cut triangles first. That is fine. The order in which they fold and cut the shapes is secondary to finding the lines

Teacher Note

It may be difficult for you to step back and wait, but this is the point where you allow the students to try and figure out ways to make the smaller sized pieces from the 3-inch squares. Walk around and observe, ask students who are experiencing success how they did it, have them demonstrate for others. Ask students who are not experiencing success yet how they folded their squares. What did they observe? They may want to observe others and copy their ideas. You may need to model folding and cutting the pieces,

Teacher Note

Did they measure the 3-inch square with a ruler? Did they use addition, subtraction, or division? Did they fold it first or estimate the size? With the triangle did they discover the midpoint of the side opposite the angle, fold and divide? Did they realize the need to have a right angle in each of the

Teacher Note

As soon as the students have reduced the size of their pattern pieces (*tumaqcat*), introduce the worksheet, "More Squares." This can be used as an ongoing design project throughout the rest of the module. As students design and create more pieces and patterns they can add to the "More Squares." The squares

Teacher Note

If the students did not suggest folding on the lines of symmetry and cutting the shapes into fourths, continue to ask if they can think of another way. Encourage the students

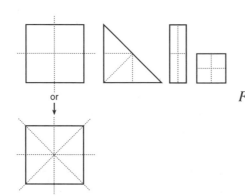

Fig. 3.9: Triangle, rectangle, small squares, the dotted lines show folding into fourths

5. Discuss with the students how they made their pieces smaller, reduced them in size, or scaled them down (see Teacher Note at top of page). Have them demonstrate and share their ideas. Record their responses on your classroom record paper.

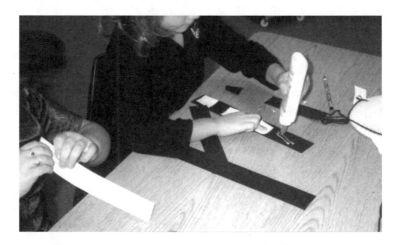

Fig. 3.10: Students making symmetrical, related pattern pieces

6. Have the students write in their notebooks and add a drawing that fits in their notebooks and is somewhat proportional, explaining their method for reducing the size of the pattern pieces.

7. Have the students store all their pattern pieces (*tumaqcat*) and scraps in their storage envelope for use in Part Two.

This may be a good place to stop for the day. Collect the storage envelopes from the students and continue with Part Two at another time.

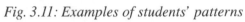

Fig. 3.11: Examples of students' patterns

Part 2: More Squares—
Creating Basic Units

The More Squares—Creating Basic Units worksheet may be started as soon as the students have completed Part 1, Activity 3, on scaling the basic square unit and other related pieces to the 1½-inch size.

Take this time to review the geometrical shapes the students have made and the relationship of the shapes to the square. Encourage your students to be creative and to go beyond the pattern pieces we have made thus far when designing each square on the worksheet. Students may leave open spaces between pieces or overlap some pieces. They will use these pieces or ideas in projects later in the module.

This activity is the first time students will have worked with shapes in two colors. It is important to stress two Yup'ik design principles here:

1.   Yup'ik designs alternate dark and light colors to make repeating patterns.
2.   Yup'ik designs are made so that the edges of the dark and light shapes match each other.

You may choose to post a copy of the worksheet in a visible place in the room and keep it as a class-recording sheet. Have students add to it as they create squares using new combinations of the pattern pieces (*tumaqcat*). For example, the first squares may be solid black and solid white. The next squares may be black and white using the triangles. If the orientation of the triangles is changed or if the colors are reversed, then new squares are created and may be posted on the classroom copy. Students may add to their own copy and keep it in their notebook. This will be an ongoing activity that may be expanded as students fold and cut their pattern pieces (*tumaqcat*) into smaller units in later activities.

Math Note

The concepts of part-whole relationships and simple fractions are embedded in this activity. As the students divide a square into smaller, congruent parts, you have an opportunity to informally teach students about fractional names and equivalents. For example, the squares in the figure are divided into halves, thirds, fourths, and ninths.

Figure 3.13 below illustrates several squares constructed according to Yup'ik design principles.

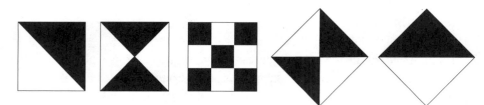

Figure 3.13. Sample squares filled with black and white pieces

Instructions

1. **Demonstrate**. Gather the students around you and show your copy of the worksheet, "More Squares—Creating Basic Units." Remind students of the parka border patterns on the poster. Ask students how many colors are used in each pattern. Then ask them how shapes of different colors are related. They should recognize that the dark and light colors always alternate, and that dark and light colored shapes always line up so that their edges match. Explain that Yup'ik pattern designers can make many different patterns using these two basic principles.

2. Take out the storage envelope with the scaled-down pieces that were made yesterday. Explain that today the students are going to create their own designs inside a square by gluing black and white pattern pieces into squares on their worksheets. Demonstrate a few ways you created a square unit using your *tumaqcat* pieces. Glue one or two of your simple square units to the worksheet. Make another copy of your first square units and rotate them 90 degrees or 180 degrees and glue them to the worksheet. Ask why they are new squares. Allow time for the students to think and explain their answers to a partner. Assist the students in realizing that different colors, sizes, and orientation of their pattern pieces qualify as new squares. By changing the attributes you have a new pattern.

3. Make conjectures. Next, ask the students to look at the square you made using a black and a white triangle. Ask what relationship the black triangle has to the square? What is its relationship to the white triangle? Have a discussion about fractions at this point. The amount of area covered by each triangle is what fraction or portion of the whole? Also, how many of the shapes or pieces are needed to cover the same area as the square? Ask the students to prove their conjectures.

4. **Demonstrate.** Cut a square into two large triangles, as shown in Figure 3.12 of the Math Note. Cut another square into two rectangles, as shown. Ask the students what the relationship is between the large triangle and the large rectangle. What portion of the area is covered by one of the triangles or one of the rectangles? (Each is equal to one half the area of the square.)

Students explore area and

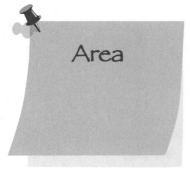

Area

As a proof, you or your students may want to cut the triangle to fit onto the rectangle, or vice versa. Repeat the process with the smaller triangles and squares. (One small triangle and one small square are equal to one fourth the area of the square.)

5. Explain. Distribute the More Squares—Creating Basic Units worksheet. Tell the students that they will be keeping a record on the worksheet of all the different ways they can form a square, using the tumaqcat pieces scaled to the 1½-inch square. They may use crayon or pencil to shade in their squares, or glue actual pieces on the worksheet. They may make different symmetrical shapes and tumaqcat pieces of their own design. Encourage them to work with their partners to make several different squares and record their squares on the worksheet.

6. Create. Allow time for students to create squares using combinations of the *tumaqcat* pieces. Have them share their squares and compare their combinations with a partner.

7. Share. Ask for volunteers to share their combinations with the class by creating them on the overhead or drawing them on the board.

8. Explain to students that during the rest of the module they will create their own repeating patterns using one or more of the squares they have created in this activity. They may record the patterns in their notebooks, on recording paper, or they may glue their *tumaqcat* pieces on construction paper to make a record of pleasing patterns.

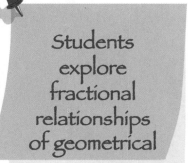

Students explore fractional relationships of geometrical

Fig. 3.14: A set of pattern squares by a student in Nenana, Alaska

Assessment

This is a good time to examine students' pattern squares to see if they understand Yup'ik design principles. Have they alternated dark and light shapes? Did they cut their dark and light shapes so they are the same? Are the shapes placed so that the edges match? If students are not demonstrating these in their designs, you may want to review them before they make their bookmarks.

Extension Activity

9. **Explore.** Allow time for the students to explore the relationship of the other *tumaqcat* pieces to each other and to the square. Students may create a puzzle by cutting symmetrical pieces from a square, arranging the pieces into another shape or configuration and outlining the shape. Some examples are shown in Figure 3.15. Then ask students to give a drawn outline of their puzzle to a partner. The partner then fills in the shape with the pieces, covering the same area. Partners then decide which covers more area—the original square, or the pieces used to cover the puzzle, or if they cover the same area. Ask for volunteers to share their ideas with the class. Ask them to prove their conjectures.

> Puzzles: Area and geometric relationships

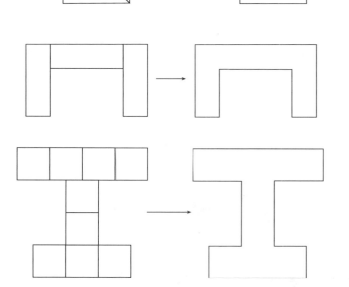

Fig. 3.15: Sample puzzles made by cutting a square into smaller congruent pieces and rearranging them. Students draw an outline, remove the pieces, and ask a friend to first fill in the puzzle, and then rearrange the pieces into a square.

Fig. 3.16: Student making a bookmark

Teacher Note

Nancy Sharp encouraged her students to create a pattern uniquely their own, using the shapes and pattern pieces they had studied, or by creating new symmetrical pattern pieces from a square. Sharp stressed students' creativity: "Some of you did slightly different ones and some of you cut these out. Now, this morning, can you make different ones? I'm going to give you this. Can you make a different shape? Who can make one? . . . but you have to think about it, you know, not waste. Don't waste, because we will use these, we'll put them in here. What are you going to make? What are you going to make? First, tell us. How are you going to make it?"

Fig. 3.17: Bookmarks made by Nancy Sharp's students

Teacher Note

According to Yup'ik design principles, border patterns are made using alternating dark and light shapes. To encourage students to follow these principles, we suggest that you offer them strips of a third color, such as yellow, red or tan to use as the "backing material" for their bookmarks. The students can cut black and white *tumaqcat* pieces and glue the pieces with sides touching. Eventually, none of the background colors will show. The teacher may assess the symmetry of the patterns and the students' ability to cut the pieces evenly and fit them snuggly together on the bookmark as shown in Figure 3.18A below.

Some students may prefer to use either a black or a white strip as the backing for the bookmark, and use *tumaqcat* shapes of the opposite color to make the pattern. For these patterns – which are simpler for less experienced students to construct – the backing material becomes part of the pattern. That is, the voids, or negative spaces not covered by their *tumaqcat* pieces, are visible. Such patterns are less reliant on the students' ability to cut and fit small pieces together, and therefore tend to be more personal, expansive, open ended and creative—although less likely to reflect Yup'ik design principles. If students create patterns this way the negative space becomes an intricate part of the pattern and should not be seen as a mistake. An example is shown in Figure 3.18B.

As you evaluate your students' abilities, it is important to encourage them by accepting the patterns they construct, without judgment. You can, however, continue to model using both dark and light shapes, and ask students if they can tell the difference between how you constructed your pattern and how they constructed theirs.

A.

B.

Fig. 3.18: Pattern A was constructed in the Yup'ik fashion, using alternating dark and light pieces
Pattern B, which looks similar, was constructed using dark triangles on a light background. The relationship between the dark and light shapes are less precise in Pattern B than in Pattern A.

Part 3: Making the Bookmark

Making the bookmarks is an inspiring, powerful moment in this module. This is where the mathematics of the shapes is merged with the creativity of the individuals to produce a wonderful array of patterns. By emulating the Yup'ik elders and engaging in joint productive activity (Lipka et al., 2005), a teacher points the direction rather than guiding the students in their learning. For example, Nancy Sharp, a teacher who taught this module, worked in parallel, joint activity with her students as a way to show how important the activity was, and encouraged creativity as the whole class engaged in creating their bookmarks. Students observe as teachers create bookmarks. When students feels ready to make their own pattern and bookmark, they may take the materials they feel they will need and go to their own work areas and begin. If a student feels a need for clarification, or more direction, he or she will consult with other students or the teacher, and observe the teacher and other students as they continue to work.

We suggest heightening student learning through cognitive apprenticeship. Although the traditional Yup'ik process of making pattern pieces through folding along lines of symmetry may have been familiar to the children, the naming and explicit mathematical properties of different mathematical shapes are necessary components for school learning. As described by Collins, Brown, and Newman (1989) and Lee (1995), a goal of cognitive apprenticeship is to enable learners to undertake complex tasks independently, often with the support of peers. Nancy Sharp prepared her students for independence and "released" them into productive work groups once she and other students had modeled various aspects of

Math Note

In order for a pattern to have a line of symmetry, the colors as well as the shapes in the pattern must match exactly when the pattern is folded across the line of symmetry. In Figure 3.19 below, pattern A, has a line of symmetry, while pattern B, which looks almost the same except for the starting and ending shapes, does not. There is no way to fold pattern B so that the shapes match when the pattern strip is folded on the center line. Students will learn how to identify lines of symmetry in patterns in Activities 5 and 6.

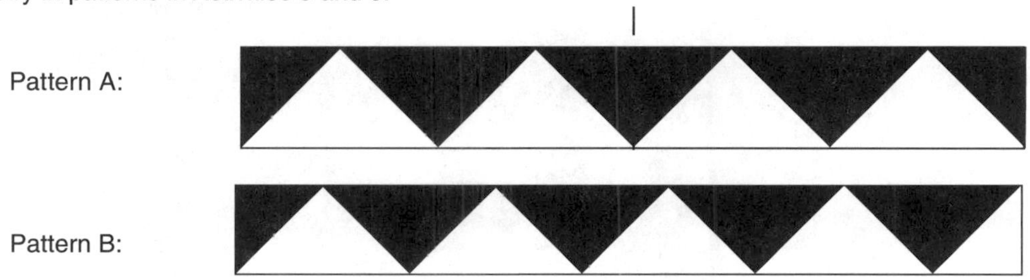

Pattern A:

Pattern B:

Fig. 3.19: Pattern A has a line of symmetry; Pattern B does not.

As the students feel ready to begin their own work, encourage them to choose one of their square designs to use for their bookmarks. Allow students time for creation of unique patterns. They may use pattern pieces in their envelopes or cut

making pattern pieces. As noted above, the beginning of independent work was signaled by culturally salient transition to joint activity. Figure 3.20 shows the students and Nancy Sharp engaged in joint productive activity.

Have precut black and white construction paper (1½ inches by 3 inches) the students can fold and cut easily, and 12 inches by 2½ inches strips available in a different color for students to use as bookmark backing. You and the students can make *tumaqcat* pieces as needed and construct one or more bookmarks.

Instructions

1. Show. Gather the students in a discussion area and point out the traditional border patters on the Yup'ik Border Patterns poster. Share the information about the names and designs of the patterns. Ask the students to identify the shapes and pieces used and describe how the shapes and patterns repeat.

2. **Discuss.** Tell them that now that we have made the pattern pieces (*tumaqcat*), and know how they relate to the square, we will be making a repeating border pattern to put on a bookmark using the reduced size pattern pieces (*tumaqcat*) based on the 1½-inch squares they made in Parts 1 and 2.

3. Explain that today they will create their own original pattern that is balanced (light and dark). They will name their pattern, and explain why they chose that name. Distribute the storage envelopes collected at the end of Part 2.

4. **Demonstrate.** Share a simple square design you have created and recorded in your notebook or on your More Squares—Creating the Basic Units worksheet that you would like to use for your bookmark. Explain to students that you are going to make a repeating pattern using the square you have chosen as a repeating element. This means that you will make many copies of your square and place them next to each other.

> ### Teacher Note
>
> Now or later, brainstorm items the students might like to decorate with a border pattern. Keep a list and when possible incorporate the students' ideas in free time activities. Some ideas include notebook cov-

Fig. 3.20: Joint productive activity

5. Joint activity. Begin working on your own bookmark, cutting your pieces and placing all of them on the background material before you start gluing them down. When your bookmark is complete, tell the students what you named the pattern and why. Ask the students if they can see at least one line of symmetry in your pattern, and make a conjecture where that line of symmetry runs in the pattern. Then fold your pattern to prove or disprove the conjecture.

6. When students' repeating patterns are established, have the students glue the pieces on the bookmark background material. Allow time for the students to make one or more bookmarks.

7. Share. Have students share their bookmarks with others, explaining the pattern, what they named it, which square they used, how they made the pattern, and what pattern pieces (*tumaqcat*) they used.

8. **Math notebooks.** Ask students to write in their notebooks about the traditional patterns, their own patterns, and what they named the patterns. Have the students explain how they made their patterns. You may want to have them record their patterns on the recording paper and include them in their notebooks. Have them store pattern pieces (*tumaqcat*) and any scraps in their envelopes for use in later activities.

Fig. 3.21: Nancy Sharp displays her finished bookmark

9. Have the students put their names on the backs of the bookmarks. Collect the bookmarks and envelopes. Keep the bookmarks for use in Activities 4 and 5. Later the bookmarks may be laminated and used, displayed, or sent home.

Assessment

Examine bookmarks for the use of Yup'ik design principles. Do they contain a repeating pattern, alternating dark and light shapes? Do the edges of the shapes match, or are there gaps between shapes? Can students determine whether their patterns have a line of symmetry?

Read notebooks for indications of knowledge of the traditional patterns, their names and meanings. Note student thinking about how they made their own patterns and what they named them.

More Squares—Creating Basic Units

Activity 4
Using a Pattern Strip
for Measuring Lengths

The use of body measures and nonstandard measures occurs in everyday life across many cultural groups. Yup'ik people such as Frederick George of Akiachak, Alaska, are quite creative in their use of everyday objects as measuring tools. In this way, today's lesson uses students' bookmarks as such a tool.

In this activity students use the bookmark patterns they made during Activity 3 as measuring tools to measure distances in the classroom. This will help them choose locations when they create a border pattern in the classroom for Activity 6. They will explore several aspects of length measurement. They will measure lengths that are longer than their bookmarks, answering questions such as how many bookmarks wide is the door of the classroom? How many bookmarks high is our bulletin board? They will recognize that these measurements are nonstandard, that is, they are not using feet and inches or meters and centimeters, which are examples of standard units. Nonstandard units can be converted into standard units (thus they are directly comparable or proportional) but that is beyond the scope of this module. If the students' bookmarks are not all the same length, then the measurements recorded using one bookmark, may not be the same using a different bookmark. This is another way in which they are nonstandard.

Students will also work to express their measurements in smaller units, using the number of repeating patterns in each bookmark as a smaller unit of length. In effect, they will be using multiplication (repeated addition) to convert measurements in bookmark lengths to measurements in repeating units. For example, if a bookmark includes four repeating units, then a distance that is seven bookmarks long can also be represented as twenty-eight repeating units long. Again, these are nonstandard units as the number of repeating units may differ from bookmark to bookmark, but comparable to measuring say in feet and then converting to inches.

> Connecting repeating patterns to repeating units in measuring

Goals
*   To measure different lengths in the classroom using a pattern strip as a ruler
*   To compute length measurements in terms of the number of repeating units

Materials
*   Completed bookmarks from Activity 3
*   Math notebooks
*   Worksheet, Measuring with a Bookmark

Duration

One class period.

Vocabulary

Estimation of length—making a reasoned guess of a length based on careful observation and prior experience.

Repeating unit—a shape or collection of shapes that is repeated to make a linear pattern.

Ruler—a standardized tool used for measuring length.

Unit of measure—a scale used to record measurements of length, area, temperature, etc.

Preparation

Use the bookmark you created in Activity 3 and practice measuring some classroom objects so that you can model the process for your students.

Instructions

1. Tell the students that today they will use their bookmarks as rulers to measure objects in the classroom. Remind them of other experiences they have had with measuring lengths. Explain that later in the module they will be creating border patterns for different areas of the classroom and that in order to know how much material they are going to need, they will need to measure the places in the classroom where the borders will be located.

2. Call students attention to one easily visible, and easily measured, length in the classroom (for example, the width of a window). Ask students to estimate how many of their bookmarks would fit end to end along the length of that object. Explain that an estimate is a guess based on carefully looking at both the ruler (their bookmark) and the distance to be measured. Invite several students to estimate the length in terms of their own bookmark.

3. Model. Invite a student volunteer to work with you to make an actual measurement. Invite the class to gather near the object you are measuring. Show students that it is helpful to have a team of two people to do the measuring. One person holds the ruler, the other marks the end of the rule with a finger, and holds the finger in place while the second person moves the ruler. Together, count the number of times the ruler fills the length.

Math Note

This is a type of measurement that involves constructing a length by building it from smaller units. Students start with a smaller unit and build up to get the entire length. In Activity 6 they will use measurement differently by starting with an entire length and dividing it into smaller units by folding.

Math Note

Accurate measurement of a long distance with a short ruler is a skill that may take some time for your students to develop. It is best carried out in pairs. One important sub-skill is marking the end of the ruler with a mark or a finger, and moving the beginning of the ruler. A second sub-skill is keeping count of the number of times the ruler length has been repeated. The length measured in Figure 4.1 is equal to four bookmarks.

Teacher Note

Fig. 4.1: Measuring a length equal to four bookmarks

If the total length is not equal to an exact number of ruler lengths, a third sub-skill is needed to account for the partial length of the ruler using fractional measures, or smaller units, that is subdivisions of the ruler.

When a nonstandard ruler such as a bookmark is used, the length of a repeating element may provide a convenient way to subdivide the ruler. In Figure 4.2 below, the distance to be measured is between three and four ruler lengths. Since the ruler is made up of seven repeats of a basic pattern element, the length being measured approximates $3\,\frac{4}{7}$ ruler lengths.

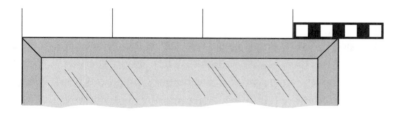

Fig. 4.2: Measuring a length using a bookmark for which smaller units are needed

If the ruler cannot easily be divided into smaller units students may prefer to approximate a length to the nearest half ruler length. In Figure 4.2 the length could be expressed as approximately $3\,\frac{1}{2}$ ruler lengths. Another approach is to make a

Teacher Note

If this is students' first experience in measuring lengths this year, this activity may take longer and require more instruction than if they have already done a lot of measuring. MCC develops students' measuring skills and concepts in the second grade

4.   Ask students to work with a partner to measure the borders of various large objects in the room. Later in the module they will choose one of these places and create a continuous border pattern around it. Brainstorm with the class to create a list of classroom objects they might want to decorate with a border pattern. Suitable objects might include the perimeter of a blackboard or bulletin board or the distance around a door or window. Assign each pair to measure two or more distances using the ruler of their choice, and make sure that each object is measured by two or more groups. Ask students to record their measurements on the worksheet, Measuring with a Bookmark.

5.   After the students have had time to make at least two measurements, record their results on a classroom chart with the same headings as the handout.

6.   Discuss with the students any differences that appear on the chart—are there different values for the same measurement? Ask students if they can explain why two groups may have gotten different measurements for the same object. They should recognize that measuring with different bookmarks could give different results depending on a) the length of the bookmark, and b) the number of small units it is divided into. Differences in the care with which different teams carry out their measurements may also account for some discrepancies. This may lead some students to appreciate the need for standard measures, and/or standardized measuring practices.

7.   **Math notebooks.** Ask students to choose one of the objects they measured and write about it in their math notebooks. They should record the measurement, explain how they determined it and note which bookmark was used. Encourage them to draw pictures as part of their explanations.

Extension Activity

8.   Your students may enjoy measuring the same objects with a standard ruler in order to determine their corresponding standard lengths. There may still be differences in the measurements reported by different groups, due to different degrees of care taken with the measurements.

Assessment
Procedures of Measuring

Read their notebooks to see whether they can describe the process they used to measure a length with bookmarks.

Observe students as they work to see if they understand how to mark the starting and endpoints of their rulers, to measure a long length. Also ask them to show you how they arrived at a particular measurement. If they subdivided their rulers to make smaller units, ask them how they decided where the subdivisions are and how they used them to measure lengths that are not equal to an exact number of ruler lengths.

Conceptual Difficulties in Measuring

Students often make the mistake of counting the starting point of a measurement as "1" instead of zero. For example, in making the measurement shown in Figure 4.3, students may start counting using the first mark at the left as "one," and therefore say that the length is equal to six bookmarks.

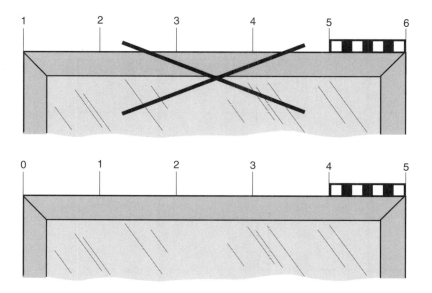

Fig. 4.3: A length measured in bookmarks. Students who count the first mark at the left as "one" may incorrectly say that the object is six book marks long instead of five.

If students subdivide a bookmark into smaller units, they may not realize that all the smaller units have to be equal in length. Also, in counting the smaller units, students might make the same type of mistake described above, and begin counting at the beginning of the bookmark with "one." At times this transfers to miscounting when they move the ruler, counting the end of the ruler and the beginning of the ruler again, thus adding an additional unit incorrectly. Such students might say that the strip in Figure 4.3 is six units long (the correct length is five units).

Finally, students may not understand why two students get different lengths when measuring the same object. One reason this can happen is that one or both students made procedural errors. Another is that they may not notice the effects of using different-sized units. If one bookmark is shorter than the other, the student using the shorter bookmark will get a larger measurement. The difference is not due to measurement error but to differences in the length of the unit used for measuring.

94

Measuring with a Bookmark

Team Members	Object Measured	Ruler Used	Length of Object

Activity 5
Finding the Basic Repeating Unit

An elder will design a pattern, make a drawing or other representation of the pattern, and analyze the pattern for balance and symmetry before cutting and sewing the pieces together. Thus, the elder or seamstress avoids making costly mistakes in a pattern where time and materials might otherwise be wasted.

In this activity, students will analyze the patterns on their bookmarks and on the Yup'ik Border Pattern poster to discover the basic repeating units. This will allow your students to understand the patterns better and will help them when they try to create their own repeating patterns.

Students will begin to identify the basic repeating unit of patterns when analyzing completed repeating patterns. The basic repeating unit of a pattern is a shape or collection of shapes (pattern pieces (*tumaqcat*)) that is repeated over and over. Students will record the basic repeating units and share them with one another. Communicating and explaining is critical to this part of the lesson because these processes may help other students to understand basic repeating units in new ways.

Earlier, students explored lines of symmetry in simple shapes. In this activity they apply what they have learned to patterns in two colors by identifying lines of symmetry in the basic repeating units. In the next activity, they will extend their understanding of symmetry in patterns by applying the concept to an entire pattern strip.

Goals
- To identify, describe, and record the basic repeating units of linear patterns
- To identify, describe, and record lines of symmetry for basic repeating units
- To recognize, describe, and extend linear patterns
- To describe how repeating linear patterns are generated

Materials
- Completed bookmarks made in Activity 3
- Handout, Yup'ik Border Patterns (*Tumaqcat Wall'u Kepuqcat*)
- Math notebooks
- Poster, Yup'ik Border Patterns (*Tumaqcat wall'u Kepuqcat*)
- Precut pattern pieces (*tumaqcat*), all shapes and sizes
- Storage envelopes
- Transparencies of students' bookmarks made in Activity 3, optional

- Transparency of the teacher's bookmark from Activity 3 (optional)
- Transparencies, What's Missing? Part 1 and Part 2
- Transparencies, What's Next? Part 1 and Part 2
- Worksheet, Recording Paper from Activity 1
- Worksheets, What's Missing? Part 1 and Part 2
- Worksheets, What's Next? Part 1 and Part 2

Duration
One to three class periods.

Vocabulary
Basic repeating unit—a shape or collection of shapes that, when repeatedly copied and moved, make up a pattern. Basic repeating unit refers to the smallest set of shapes that can be used to generate an entire pattern. (*See* Linear Pattern, Two-dimensional Pattern)

Conjecture—a statement about a mathematical fact, relationship, or generalization that is based on careful observation or experimentation but which has not been proven. (See Proof)

Line of symmetry—a line that is a property of a geometric figure (a shape, design, or pattern); it divides the figure into two equal parts such that when the figure is reflected about that line, the result is identical to the starting figure. For example, a square has four lines of symmetry: one vertical, one horizontal, and two diagonal lines through the center. An informal test for a line of symmetry in a two-dimensional shape is to fold the shape along a line through its center. If both sides match exactly after folding, the line is a line of symmetry.

Proof—a mathematical argument, based on logical reasoning, that demonstrates that a particular fact or relationship is true. (See Conjecture)

Preparation
Use the bookmark you created in Activity 3 or complete a simple pattern on a bookmark and make a transparency to show the class. Select several or all of the patterns the students made on their bookmarks and reproduce them on a transparency or large display. Gather and prepare materials, including the storage envelopes from previous activities with *tumaqcat* pieces the students have made from 1½-inch squares. As before, the students may continue to make their own squares and pattern pieces. Spend more time on math and creating repeating patterns. Supply the students with precut 1½-inch squares.

Spend some time looking at the square patterns you and your students made during Activity 3 so you can help students identify lines of symmetry in patterns.

You will need the transparencies of What's Missing, Part 1 and Part 2, and What's Next, Part 1 and Part 2 to introduce the worksheets included in Part 2 of this lesson. The worksheets will help students recognize and create sequences of patterns. Some students may need to use the Yup'ik pattern pieces (*tumaqcat*) to help visualize patterns.

Part 1: Analyze patterns

Instructions

1. **Discuss and Demonstrate.** Tell the students that today we are going to analyze patterns and find the simplest, or smallest, part of the pattern that is repeated. Show the students a transparency of your bookmark on the overhead or duplicate your repeating pattern on a work area using your pattern pieces (*tumaqcat*), so that all the students can see the pattern. Ask students to identify a group of shapes that repeats over and over again to make the bookmark pattern.

Teacher Note

There may be more than one group of shapes students will identify as repeating units. Ask clarifying questions like: Which shapes were used, how many of each, and in which order were they used? Allow a few minutes for partners to share their ideas with each other and then ask for volunteers to share with the class. When a response is offered by the students, do not immediately agree, but ask, "Does

---

2. Now ask students to find the smallest combination of shapes that can be used over and over again to make the entire bookmark pattern. (Use the samples provided in Figure 5.1 or use samples from students' bookmarks.) Explain that this is called the basic repeating unit for the pattern. Have volunteers come to the overhead and use the transparency of your bookmark pattern to show their ideas of the basic repeating unit for your bookmark and explain their responses. Again, ask if the rest of the class agrees and ask if there is a different shape combination that could also be the basic repeating unit for the bookmark pattern.

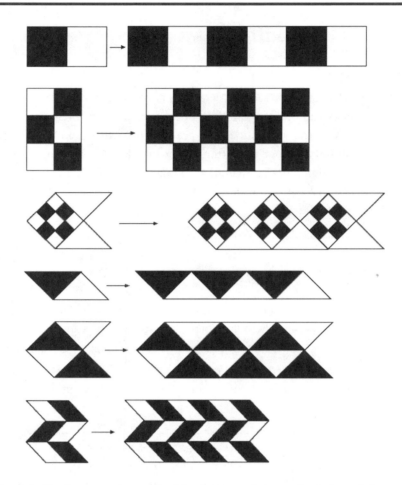

Fig. 5.1: Basic repeating units. The basic unit is on the left and the corresponding repeating patterns are on the right. Each one is repeated three times.

3. Exploring symmetry. Ask students to make a conjecture about whether the basic repeating element has one or more lines of symmetry. Ask students to draw the line(s) of symmetry on the overhead transparency of your bookmark's basic repeating unit. Ask them how they could test to find out if the basic repeating unit has a line of symmetry. (They should suggest cutting out a basic repeating element and folding it on a line through the middle to see if both halves match exactly.) Point out that when they test a black and white pattern for symmetry, both the shapes and the black and white colors in the pattern must match.

Teacher Note

When analyzing repeating patterns, allow the students to make a basic unit and repeat it several times. Does it match the pattern being analyzed? Is this pattern the same as the one you were trying to construct? If it does not match, allow the

Math Note

The figures below illustrate two simple repeating patterns and two or more basic repeating elements for each one.

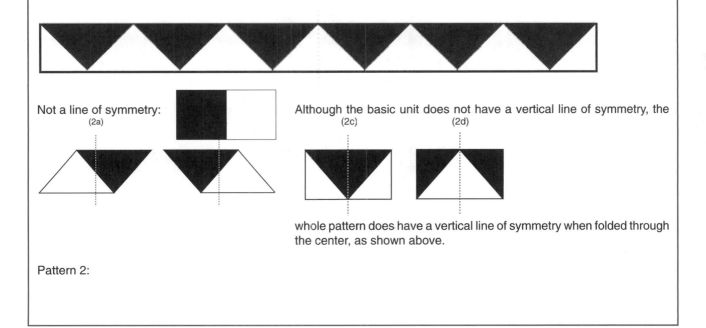

Pattern 1:

Basic repeating units:

(1a)   (1b)

In order for a pattern or design to have a line of symmetry, the colors in the pattern must match across the line of symmetry as well as the shapes. In some cases one of the basic repeating units for a pattern may have a line of symmetry, while a different repeating element for the same pattern may not have one. For Pattern 1 above, both repeating units 1A and 1B have horizontal lines of symmetry.

Students may think that the units have vertical lines of symmetry as well. Have them fold these patterns across their vertical center lines to show that the black and white colors do not match, even though the black and white squares are congruent.

Not a line of symmetry: Although the basic unit does not have a vertical line of symmetry, the
(2a)   (2c)   (2d)

whole pattern does have a vertical line of symmetry when folded through the center, as shown above.

Pattern 2:

4. Distribute the bookmarks made in Activity 3 (and the storage envelopes with the students' *tumaqcat* pieces if you have not already done so). Have other pattern pieces available as needed. Ask the students to work in pairs and use the *tumaqcat* pieces in their storage envelopes to demonstrate how they made their basic repeating unit and pattern.

5. Proof. Have the students describe their basic repeating units to a partner. Have the students make a conjecture and offer proof about a line of symmetry. (Walk around and observe each student, noting their explanation of their basic units and lines of symmetry. This may take considerable time, depending on the size of your class. Have students rotate partners and share their ideas with several people.)

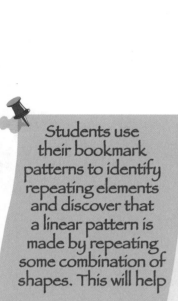

Students use their bookmark patterns to identify repeating elements and discover that a linear pattern is made by repeating some combination of shapes. This will help

6. **Discuss.** Ask for volunteers to show the transparency of their bookmark pattern on the overhead and point out the basic repeating unit they identified to the class. Discuss why they selected the basic (smallest) repeating unit and where it is repeated in their patterns. Have them show the lines of symmetry they proved. Allow thinking and sharing time.

7. If more practice is needed, distribute copies of the Yup'ik Border Patterns handout and ask students to identify the basic repeating unit of each pattern. Ask if they can find any lines of symmetry in the repeating units they identify.

8. **Math notebook.** Have the students record their basic repeating units and other students' basic repeating units they liked, with lines of symmetry, in their notebooks or on recording paper. Explain that they may want to use these pleasing patterns later.

9. Collect their notebooks and storage envelopes.

Extension Activity

10. Provide time and materials for students to design patterns. Set up a center or allow students to maintain a supply of pattern pieces (*tumaqcat*) at their desk or work area. Allow free exploration of patterns. The students may record any pleasing pattern they make or see to use in the next activities.

Provide a template in the form of a linear pattern grid for students to record the patterns they create. For example, see Figure 5.2.

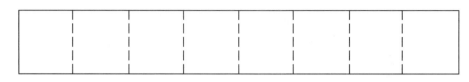

Fig. 5.2: Linear pattern grid template

Assessment

Read notebooks for indications that students can identify the basic repeating units of their bookmark patterns and the symmetry of the units or patterns.

Can students find the unit that repeats? Can they find a repeating pattern? Can they find the basic repeating unit (the smallest pattern that repeats)? Can students describe the repeating pattern in more than one way? Can they identify and show lines of symmetry—by folding, using a mirror, using logical reasoning?

In the next part of this activity, the What's Missing? and What's Next? worksheets can also help you assess students' understandings about repeating linear patterns.

Part 2: What's Missing? and What's Next?

These worksheets will help students consolidate their understanding of what makes a linear repeating pattern and will also allow you to assess that understanding at a glance. The "What's Missing?" exercise will help students observe patterns and recognize missing parts. "What's Next?" will help students learn to extend a pattern that has already been started. Both will help you assess whether students can identify basic repeating elements in linear patterns.

Instructions

1. Show a transparency of What's Missing? Part 1. In each of the four patterns, something is missing. Invite a volunteer to show the class which parts they would fill in for the first example.

2. Distribute copies of What's Missing? Part 1 and Part 2. Students can use their pattern pieces (*tumaqcat*) and glue them in or they may use pencils to draw in the missing parts. Those who finish may color the patterns.

3. Invite volunteers to show their results to the class by coloring in the missing parts of Part 1 patterns 2–4, and Part 2.

4. The What's Next? worksheet can be approached the same way. You may want to model the process using a transparency for the first example before giving students time to work. After students have had time to work and have checked their results with their partners, invite volunteers to draw their results on the overhead transparencies.

5. Continue to provide time and materials for students to design patterns. Set up a center or allow students to keep a supply of pattern pieces (*tumaqcat*) at their desk or work area. Allow free exploration of patterns. The students may record any pleasing pattern they make or see to use in the next activities.

6. Invite students to make their own What's Missing? or What's Next? puzzles for their classmates, starting by making any linear repeating pattern they like, then drawing a copy of the pattern, leaving out part in the middle with space to fill in, or start with two or three of the basic repeating elements and leave a blank space for their classmates to fill in the rest of the pattern.

Assessment

Collect the students' worksheets and examine them for correct solutions. If you find incorrect solutions, you may be able to consolidate the students' understandings by displaying one or more incorrect solutions on a transparency (without identifying the students who made them) and ask the class if they think this is correct. If not, why not? How could they fix it?

Name_____ Date _____

What's Missing? Part 1

Here are some repeating patterns. Something is missing in each pattern. Use your pencil to fill in the missing part. Color the patterns if you wish.

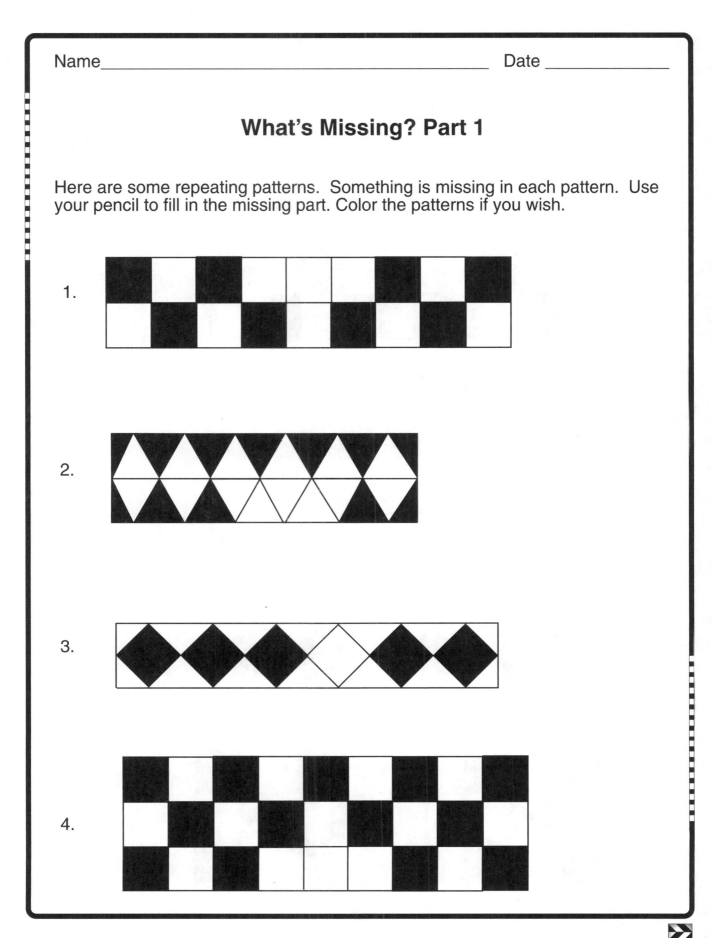

1.

2.

3.

4.

Name_____ Date _____

What's Missing? Part 2

Here are some repeating patterns. Something is missing in each pattern. Use your pencil to fill in the missing part. Color the patterns if you wish.

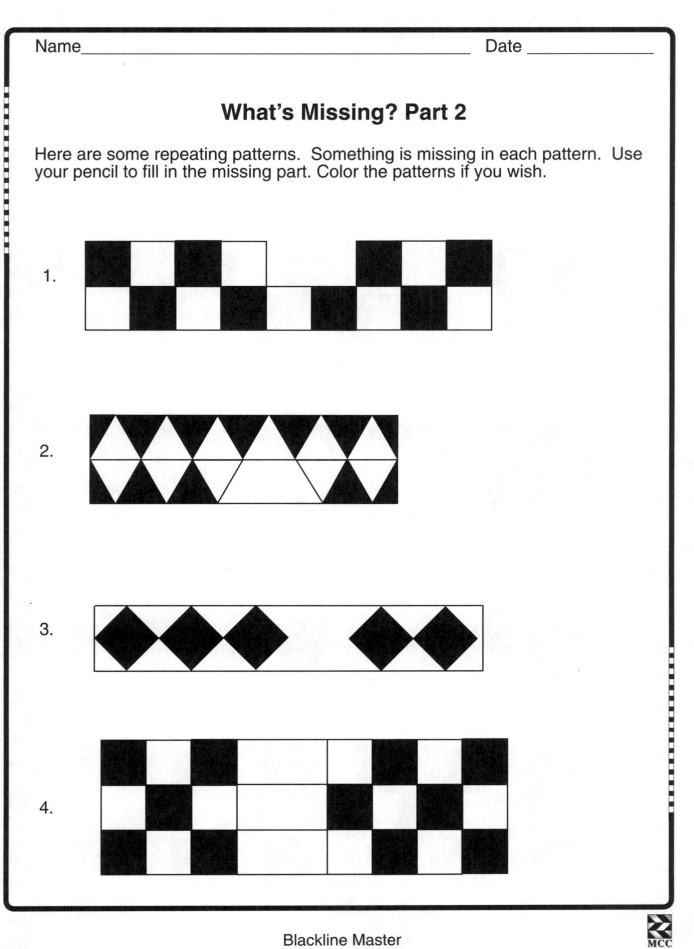

1.

2.

3.

4.

MCC

Name _____

Date _____

What's Next? Part I

Here are some designs. Use your pencil to repeat each design as many times as will fit the paper.

You may color the patterns if you wish, but be sure to follow the pattern

1.

2.

3.

What's Next? Part 2

Name _____

Date _____

4.

5.

6.

MCC

Activity 6
Making Continuous Borders

Your students have had practice creating and designing repeating patterns starting with the basic unit first. Yup'ik elders begin by thinking of the end product first, the whole or the parka, visualizing the border and the partitioning of the border, which then dictates the size of the original square unit used for creating all the pattern pieces (*tumaqcat*).

In this activity, your students will make continuous borders using the same process the elders use, by planning a design with a finished product in mind. In Part 1, the entire class will make a border for a section of the classroom or hall, using one of the places they measured in Activity 4, first by creating a square unit of measure to fit that location. Then the entire class will agree on a pattern and collaborate in making the pieces and assembling the pattern. In Part 2, the students will follow the process of the elders as they make creative borders for their individual parkas. They will apply what they learned about measuring, partitioning, scaling, and basic repeating patterns. Each student will make and complete his or her own pattern design.

When making a decorative border to apply to a parka or other objects, first you have to make a decision about the size of the basic square unit. This is important because using a square that is too large for the object being decorated makes it awkward to fit onto the object. Using a square unit that is too small requires sewing tiny pieces. Visualizing and estimating a square that will be the appropriate size takes practice and skill.

*Fig. 6.1: Pretend windows (*egeleruat*) design on a parka*

Goals
* To measure a distance and partition it into sections
* To work collaboratively to produce a repeating pattern and a continuous border
* To investigate the symmetry or balance of a pattern strip

Materials
* Adding machine tape or some other continuous strip of paper for measuring and partitioning
* Construction paper, black and white
* Glue sticks
* Math notebooks
* Posters, Yup'ik Parkas with Patterns, or a real parka if available
* Storage envelopes
* Scissors

Duration

Three to four class periods.

Vocabulary

Area—the amount of surface covered by a shape or region. Area is most often measured in square units appropriate to the size of the shape or region, such as square inches, square yards, square miles, and so forth.

Linear pattern—a one-dimensional (potentially) infinite pattern which repeats a basic unit (geometric shape or design) over and over again, such as in a band, border pattern, or strip pattern. These are sometimes called "frieze patterns" because of their use in architectural settings.

Review all other vocabulary covered in the module as needed. Encourage students to use the vocabulary in math conversations and in their notebook writing.

Preparation

Gather and prepare materials. Help students choose an area of the school to decorate with a continuous border. If you have worked through Section 2, Explorations A–D outside of math time, the students will have a completed parka and be ready to apply the border.

After you have completed Part 1, step 7, prepare strips of construction paper in two colors for students to use to make pattern pieces, and another strip of a different color to use for the background.

Read the assessment on page 111 as a guide to facilitate students' mathematical thinking and assess their construction of a repeating unit.

Part 1: Creating a Classroom Design

Instructions

1. Explain to your students that they will use the *tumaqcat* pieces to create a pleasing pattern for a border in the location you and the students agree on. They will then have a few minutes to explore patterns that they find pleasing and will agree on single pattern. Work with the students to choose one of the locations they measured during Activity 4 for the class border pattern. It should be large enough so that all the students can be involved in making the pattern.

2. Joint Activity. Distribute the students' storage envelopes and encourage students to create a pattern they would like everyone to use. Start creating a pattern of your own while students work in small groups. This activity empasizes creating and selecting a design. Later students will replicate the

design in a larger size. Invite students to observe others' work. Circulate and discuss the patterns the students have made.

3. Have students share their patterns with their groups. Each group will select one pattern for consideration.

4. Display the selected patterns and discuss the designs. Are they simple or complex? Are there a lot of big shapes or a lot of little shapes? Which look pleasing? Have the class select a single pattern for their border.

5. Hold up one of the 1 ½-inch squares used in previous activities. Ask the students if they think the square is the right size for the project. They may notice that it might be a bit small and would take a long time to complete the border. The size of the square will depend on the width of the background strip. **Hint:** Smaller squares will take longer to decorate a continuous border than larger squares. Suggest they stay in the 3 to 12 inch range. Remind students that a pattern with squares turned at a 45-degree angle will need squares of a different size than a pattern in which the squares are horizontal. After deciding on a size, measure the square so students can cut and prepare background strips.

6. Work with the class to measure the length of the area to be decorated. Determine the entire length first and divide it into equal sections so that each group will have approximately the same amount of space to decorate with the selected pattern. **Hint:** Using adding machine tape is one way to measure the wall. Have the students unroll the tape along the wall and cut it to the appropriate length. Then the students can fold the tape into the same number of parts as there are groups of students in the class. You can simplify this process by dividing the class ahead of time into three, four, or eight groups. It will be easier to fold the tape in thirds, quarters, or eighths so that each group has approximately the same length to decorate.

Once each group has a length of tape, they can divide the tape into equal portions so that each student has the same length to decorate.

> # Teacher Note
>
> As you and your students work through the process of deciding on one pattern for the entire class to construct, help them choose a basic pattern design that is interesting to them.

Fig. 6.2: Girl working on a pattern

Teacher Note

This may be a good place to stop for the day. It may be useful to prepare the background materials and the black and white strips of construction paper by cutting them

---

7. Distribute the prepared materials and assign each group to one section of the border. The students will use problem solving skills to create enough pattern pieces (*tumaqcat*) for the whole group. They may create a table and then do production line processing to make the number of pieces required

Teacher Note

This is a large assignment and is one of the culminating activities. Pose questions to individuals, pairs, small groups, or the whole class. How will the students organize and manage their materials? Should they make enough pattern pieces to cover their entire section first, or do they cut and paste as they go? What kind of planning are they doing? How will they combine their collective work to have a smooth transition from one student's section to

by the group. It is important to maintain the size and symmetry of the pattern on the border background and make sure that each section will meet and match the next section.

As students work, display the agreed-upon pattern on the overhead. Allow time (this may take more than one day) for the groups to complete their sections, modeling and helping each other as needed.

8. Ask students to estimate the number of basic repeating elements that each student will need to complete their own section of the pattern. Then ask students to determine the number of copies of each dark and light shape they will need.

9. Put up the border strips as they are completed. Continually encourage students to observe the pattern as it grows. Ask them to conjecture about whether they will succeed in connecting the pattern without a gap or an overlap.

10. Have students create a table looking at the finished project, including
    • how many strips were needed to cover the border
    • how many repeating units
    • how many of each dark or light shape

Math Note

This activity introduces two new elements of linear patterns: the need for end or "turning" squares and the need to decide on the orientation of the pattern strips.

Suppose the class decides to construct a pattern around a bulletin board, as shown in Figures 6.3 and 6.4. The pattern will run along the top, sides, and bottom of the bulletin board. The class will have to decide how to orient the pattern along each edge, including the corner squares, where the pattern changes direction. In Figure 6.3 below, the pattern is arranged so that the dark triangles always "point in" to the center of the space, and the corner squares have been made light colored. It could have been dark, or shaded along a diagonal. In Figure 6.4, the dark triangles always point downward, and the corner squares are the same as all the others. The decision about how to do this is a matter of taste, but for consistency, the class must decide.

Fig 6.3: Sample A: The dark triangles

Fig. 6.4: Sample B: The dark triangles

11. **Math notebooks.** Have the students make a notebook entry based on the tasks they performed to complete the border and the math they used to accomplish it.

Assessment

Assess student understanding of the main ideas of the module through notebook entries, observations, and discussion. You can reassess at the end of Part 2. Refer to the Math Notes in the Module Overview for more detailed descriptions of these concepts. Suggestions for assessment include:

1. Creating shapes by dividing a basic square
   * Do students divide the square along its lines of symmetry?
   * Do they divide it into congruent shapes?
2. Listing names and properties of the triangles and quadrilaterals they use for their basic shapes
   * Can students identify number of sides, number of angles, number of equal sides and equal angles, and lines of symmetry?
3. Creating a repeating unit
   * Does the repeating unit balance dark and light shapes?
   * Do the edges of the shapes match?
   * Can students identify lines of symmetry in their repeating units?
4. Determining how many copies of each shape are needed
   * Can students determine how many basic repeating units are needed for each section of the border pattern?
   * Can they find how many of each dark and light shape are needed by "multiplying" the number of shapes in the repeating unit by the number needed (multiplication may involve skip counting, repeated addition, making a table, etc.)?
5. Identifying lines of symmetry in the repeating unit and in the pattern as a whole
   * What tools or strategies do students use to identify lines of symmetry (folding, mirrors, visual comparison across a center line, etc.)?
   * Do students recognize that the colors and shapes must both match across the line of symmetry?
6. Measuring/partitioning the space to determine how large the repeating elements should be and how many copies of that element are needed
   * Can students divide a length into equal, smaller units?
   * Can they use the thickness of their pattern strip to determine how large their starting squares will be for the pattern?

Part 2: Creating a Parka Border

To help them gain a better understanding of symmetry, balance, and spatial visualization, students will create a repeating pattern for a parka border. The pattern may be one that you have demonstrated, a pattern they have seen elsewhere, or an original. This will be the final activity. The completion of the parka in Section 2 Explorations A–D should be planned to coincide with this lesson. Making a border to decorate the parka incorporates all the math learned to date and provides an opportunity for students to create their own patterns.

Cultural Note

As Mary Active and Annie Blue, both elders of Togiak, Alaska, worked on designs for parkas, they talked about their patterns. Evelyn Yanez, a long-term consultant to the project and a Yup'ik teacher and translator, asked: "If this piece is dark, what will this one be?" Mary Active replied: "It will be white. And if these are white, these other would be black." Then someone asked: "Why is it important to balance white and black?" "It is for the eyes," chorused the two elders. "It is to make it appealing to the eyes" (translation).

Preparation

Invite an elder to talk with the class. Obtain a real parka if possible. Before students begin working on their parka border strip, they need to have a parka ready to measure and decorate. Make sure they have completed Section 2, Explorations A-C and Exploration D Steps 1-5, so they have a parka ready to measure for a border. See page 118 for an example of a student decorating a parka.

If possible, have a parka with a border to show the students. Gather and prepare materials. Plan to share Yup'ik cultural information with students.

Instructions

1. Bring in an actual parka if available and ask an elder to talk about making a parka. How did she make the border so it would fit the parka? Did she make the parka first or the border first? Different people do it different ways.

2. **Discuss.** Tell the students that today they will finish their parkas by adding a border they will create. Explain that they will use all the ideas they have learned about Yup'ik ways of making patterns and all the mathematical ideas they have learned about repeating patterns, basic units, lines of symmetry, measuring, and estimating.

3. Review lines of symmetry. Explain that there is one more Yup'ik design approach that students will need to know before they can design their patterns. This is the principle of symmetry or balance for a repeating pattern. First ask students to recall what they already know about lines of symmetry for a shape. Use shapes the students can see in the room or hold up a square and a right isosceles triangle and ask students to show you all the lines of symmetry they can find for each shape.

Hold up a basic repeating unit for one of your patterns. Ask students to prove to you whether it does or does not have a line of symmetry.

4. Let the students know that you will be asking them how they will measure and partition their borders. Ask students to identify the design they will use and the name of the border pattern they have created. How will they describe their pattern? What are the lines of symmetry? What is the basic repeating unit? What pieces are in their basic repeating units? How many of each of those pieces will they need for one unit? How many of those basic units will be needed to go all the way around the parka? How do students plan to keep waste to a minimum? Figuring this out may take some time, so continue to circulate.

5. Distribute black and white construction paper, continuous strips of adding machine tape (long enough to go around or across the hem of their pretend parkas), scissors, and glue sticks.

6. Encourage students to make and complete the border pattern of their choice, using the designs from their notebooks.

7. As the students are working, circulate, appreciate their patterns, and comment on originality and creativity. Ask questions based on their patterns.

8. Have students put their names on the back of the borders and collect and display or keep them until the parkas are completed. (You may have them add the border to their parkas now or later.)

9. **Math notebooks.** Have students write and draw about the borders they used, how they measured the length and partitioned it, and how they created a basic unit that was then repeated to create a continuous pattern to cover the length needed.

10. Invite parents in to appreciate the students' work and what they have learned.

As students create their own parka border patterns, they will use the skills and concepts they have learned, including creating and combining shapes, creating repeating elements for two-color linear

Math Note

When Yup'ik elders construct their parka border patterns, they always try to have a line of symmetry (or a line of balance) in the center of their pattern strips. This means that if you take a pattern strip and fold it across its centerline, that line must either be a line of symmetry or a line of balance for the entire strip. You can demonstrate this using two of the Yup'ik pattern strips, pretend boxes and pretend braids. Fold the strip in half so that the two ends meet, and ask if the fold is a line of symmetry.

A. Pretend Boxes

Folding the pretend boxes pattern strip across its centerline shows that the entire strip has a line of symmetry. All the colors and all the shapes match when folded.

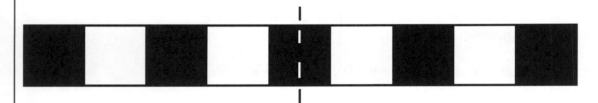

B: Pretend Braids

Pretend braids does not have a line of symmetry. If you fold it across its centerline, the shapes on the two halves do not match. However, it does have a line of balance, an idea that is very important to Yup'ik pattern makers. The number of pattern elements on both sides of the centerline are the same.

C. Pretend Boxes Variation

If you create a version of pretend boxes with a dark square on one end and a light square on the other, the pattern strip as a whole does not have a line of symmetry. If you fold the strip across its centerline, the colors will not match. However, the centerline does represent a line of balance, because the number of pattern elements is the same on both sides of the line.

Patterns and Section

Making a Parka (*Atkuk*)

In Making a Parka (*Atkuk*), students use their knowledge of symmetry and patterns to create the smaller rectangluar pieces with tassels (*nunurat*), a repeating circular border, a ruff, and a completed paper parka.

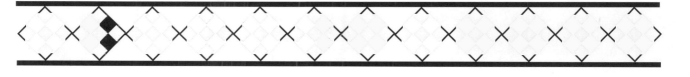

Making a Parka (*Atkuk*)

Parka Construction

In this section students will learn about the construction of a Yup'ik Eskimo parka and the cultural aspects of the use of materials. Students will work with simulated calfskin to make the smaller rectangular pieces with tassels. These pieces are located right next to each other like a belt. The larger white rectangles are part of the tassels. This part of the tassel includes family symbols. Students will create a parka with a ruff from paper and will decorate their parka with the tassels and a border pattern. Thus, we have a gathering of pieces to make a whole.

The following activities complement the math lessons. You may plan parka construction to meet the needs of your classroom. By working collaboratively with other teachers (art, social studies, bilingual, etc.), time other than math time can be used for parka construction.

Cultural Note

Mary Active talked about making a parka:

> *A long time ago when I was a young girl, my parents used to hunt for squirrels when we moved to the mountains. My mother, older sister, and father would go out hunting. Only males [squirrels] come out first. When the geese start arriving the females would start to come out. [My family] would get around 40 or near 50 squirrels. Every 52 skins were bundled for a parka. The female skins were bundled together and males another—because male skins are large. These male skins were made for the ones they loved most. I used the stomach parts that were not used in making [real] parkas [to make parkas for dolls]. (Translation)*

Anuska Nanalook of Manokotak, Alaska, explained that where she lives, they look for sea lion and sealskin. They also use calfskin because the hair is short and makes good pieces for a pattern. She, too, pointed out that the fur must be cut so it all lies in the same direction, pointing down so the parka sheds rain and snow, and that the pelt cutting must be planned so no waste occurs.

Making a parka is a time-honored tradition amongst the Yup'ik and other Alaska Native people. The work involved is extensive and time consuming. After getting the squirrels, the skins are removed and processed. Skins are dried, then soaked in a soapy solution, rubbed with both hands and stretched, and then dried again. That process is repeated until the skins are soft and white and the fur is fluffy and clean. During parka construction the seamstress may work for a short time, then put the project away and work on it later. Eventually, the parka is ready for the border to be added and a useful and functional work of art has been created: a parka. See Figure A.1.

For this module, the construction of a parka may be accomplished several ways. Students could make the entire parka in one class period or take several days or weeks. The individual pieces, (body, hood, ruff, rectangular pieces with tassels, and borders) could be made on separate days and attached to make the completed parka. One teacher had students use butcher paper to make a flat parka that could be displayed on a wall. Another teacher had students use two layers of butcher paper and make a tunic that could be worn by the students. Still other teachers had students sew parkas from felt or other materials, with other adults helping as needed. Choose a method that works for you and your students and plan accordingly so the parkas are ready to have the borders attached when you reach Activity 6.

*Fig. A.1: A traditional
        squirrel parka*

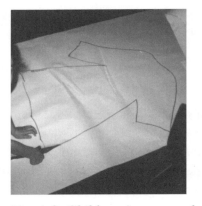

Fig. A.2: Child cutting out parka

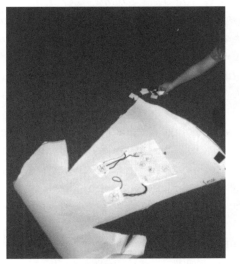

Fig. A.3: Child decorating parka

Exploration A
Preparing Calfskin

In this activity students simulate making a calfskin out of butcher paper.

Cultural Note

Before calfskin was available, ermine was used for the white part of the border. Other materials might be the belly portion of caribou skin, which is lighter, or other light color furs. The black portion of the border was made using swan's feet or other dark color furs. Swan feet are very large and the webbing between the toes was thin and durable.

Fig. A.4: Calfskin and pretend calfskin

Anuska Nanalook, an elder from Manakotak, Alaska, explained the process of selecting calfskin. She looked for calfskin with short hair rather than long hair because it is easier to cut and required less trimming. The main selection requirement was a balance of black and white areas so the border pattern could be made with a balance of light and dark. She made the final selection by finding calfskin that was thin and supple, easier to cut and sew. Small imperfections and swirls of hair (cowlicks) were noted but did not change her selection.

When cutting and sewing calfskin or other furs, the direction the hair or fur lies is very important. Fur and hair that lie downward help keep the rain and snow from soaking into the garment, which is important for staying dry and warm. Tracing and cutting on the tanned side of the calfskin, while staying within a white or black area on the front of the calfskin, takes some practice. Making sure the hair lies in the correct direction on each piece is an added problem. Incorrectly cut pieces are saved to use later.

Goals
- To make pretend calfskin (See Figure A.4)

Materials
- Black markers

- Butcher paper
- Calfskin (a sample piece is fine or another type of tanned fur) if available
- Math notebooks
- Pretend calfskin for demonstration
- Scissors

Preparation

Make a paper copy of a black and white calfskin to use for demonstration (see Figure A.4). Have enough butcher paper for each student to have approximately a one- to three-foot square piece. If you wish to share information about the Yup'ik way of life and on designing, making, and use of parkas, then visit the following Web site of the Alaska Native Heritage Center for more information about parkas: http://www.alaskanative.net/192.asp.

Instructions

1. Gather the students around you while you demonstrate.

2. Show the students the real calfskin or fur, if available.

3. **Discuss.** Talk about the front and back. Ask which side would be easier to use to trace and cut a shape. Talk about tracing and cutting on the tanned side so the hair or fur is not damaged, and that it is easier to mark and cut a straight line. Which direction should the hair or fur lie when the pieces are cut, sewn, and applied to a parka?

4. **Demonstrate.** Show the students the pretend calfskin you prepared or demonstrate how to make a pretend calfskin.

5. Have the students make a pretend calfskin with the butcher paper and black markers and write their name on the back.

6. Set this aside for use in Exploration B.

Teacher Note

During parka construction you may want the students to make notebook entries about the cultural and practical use of the parka. Entries about how the calfskin is selected, how the tassels are made, and the measuring and sewing of the parka and border may be included.

Fig. A.5: Nancy Sharp's daughter, Naparyaq Lillian Sharp Breeland, in parka

Exploration B
Creating the Rectangular Pieces and Tassels for a Ground Squirrel Parka

The students will learn a new way of measuring, and practice their visual estimation skills by creating the smaller rectangular pieces with tassels (*nunurat*), located over Annie's hands in Fig B.1. Fur hangs from both the smaller rectangular pieces (*nunurat*) and larger rectangular pieces (*qemirrlugun*) in the front and the back of the parka; the larger middle piece, which includes family symbols, is located on the front and the back of the parka. These are accompanied by two smaller pieces with additional family symbols, shown in Figure B.1.

Cultural Note

Elders Mary Active and Annie Blue sat on the floor with Annie's beautiful ground squirrel parka spread out between them. Mary said plain parkas are called *atkuut*, and Annie said:

Fig. B.1: Annie Blue's parka, front

> *Plain squirrel parka without tassels would be* alngailnguar, *"one without tassels." The fancy parka with tassels are called* alngalek, *"one with tassels." (Translation)*

The two elders talked about the the small tassels, with symbols on the center front and back tassels. They explained that different families used different materials, different numbers, and different symbols on the bound part of the small tassels.

Mary Active and Annie Blue explained that the designs on parkas worn by men are different from those worn by women. Parkas worn by men have a shoulder symbol (*tusruteq*), made of strong white caribou or calfskin, which prevents tearing. Sometimes men wear parkas that go over their heads and are not cut open in front. Sometimes the trim resembles a braid with one braid on a man's parka and two braids on a woman's parka, so from behind you can tell if the person is a man or a woman.

The importance of the symbols as family identifiers is highlighted in a story told by Annie Blue. This is a short version of "Slave Girl Escapes," which will be published in a full version.

> *A long time ago during the big Eskimo war there was a woman who was not treated right by her husband. She put her baby on her back and started walking back to her own*

Fig. B.2: Front and back tassels with the pretend bow and arrow

village. It was a long way and the weather was very cold. She could walk no farther. Finally she fell down in the snow. A man came along and saw her. The mother of the woman recognized the symbols on her parka and brought her home. She and her baby both lived. Later the husband wanted her back in his village, but her own family refused to send her back because the husband had mistreated her. (Translation)

Annie Blue's squirrel parka has six small pieces (*nunurat*), and Mary Active describes a parka with five. The number depends on their family's pattern. The small pieces (*nunurat)* are evenly spaced across the front and the back of the parka, at chest and waist level. One to three may also be placed on the sleeve.

Annie's parka has symbols for the pretend bow (*urluvruaq*) and pretend arrow (*pitegcautnguaq*) on the center front and back larger pieces. Other symbols used on the center front and back larger strips include pretend drum (*cauyaruaq*), bird claws (*cetumquruaq*), and the tip of the middle finger (*katngisnguaq*). Evelyn Yanez, an consultant to this project, commented that she could have

pretend bow and arrow - *uriuvruaq pitegcautnguaq*

pretend tip of the middle finger - *katngisnguaq*

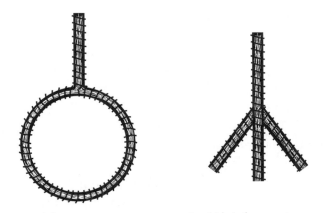

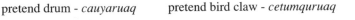

pretend drum - *cauyaruaq*   pretend bird claw - *cetumquruaq*

Fig. B.3: Four typical symbols used on parkas. Pretend bow and arrow (urluvruaq pitegcautnauaq), *pretend tip of the middle finger* (katngisnguaq), *pretend drum* (cauyaruaq), *and pretend bird claw* (cetumquruaq)

most of the above symbols, except the pretend drum (*cauyaruaq*), on her parka because she is related to each of the families who use these symbols. They also described a part of the parka (*qulitaq*) which hangs from the shoulder and includes family symbols.

Goals

*   To learn about and practice nonstandard measurement using body parts
*   To use visual estimation to determine size and shape

Materials

*   Glue
*   Math notebooks
*   Parka or doll wearing a parka if available
*   Pretend calfskins from Exploration A
*   Sample of the tassels
*   Scissors
*   Transparency, Annie Blue's Parka, Back
*   Transparency, Annie Blue's Parka, Front
*   Yarn: red, black, and white

Preparation

Make the small pieces and the larger ones to show the class. Gather materials. Plan how to share Yup'ik information, including Annie Blue's story, with students.

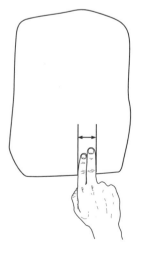 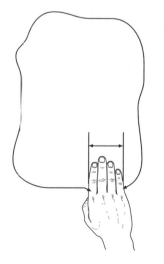

Fig. B.4: Two-finger measure   *Fig. B.5: Four-finger measure*

Instructions

1. Show the class the transparencies of Annie Blue's parka. Have them observe the pattern she used on the small pieces and the larger pieces. Explain the hard work that people must do to obtain or process traditional materials and that they will save all their scraps and not waste materials. If possible, bring in an actual parka.

2. Show students the small pieces you have made and explain where they belong on a parka.

   Different people make the tassels in different ways. Some people cut a piece of calfskin three or four fingers wide and four fingers long. Then, after adding the decoration, they fold the width around a finger to make a tube to create the small tassels with the red yarn and tuffs of wolf sewn on the inside of the tube. Other people cut the calfskin pieces one to four fingers wide and four fingers long and do not fold them. The students can use either method they choose.

*Fig. B.6: Annie Blue's
parka, back*

3. Show the students your pretend calfskin. Tell them that they will be making some small tassels and center front and back tassels for a parka.

4. First, demonstrate how to estimate how many pieces you will need. Use two fingers to estimate the number of small tassels each parka will need. Use four fingers to estimate the number of center front and back tassels needed.

5. Cut out more pieces. Use the first piece as a template for the rest, trying not to waste the material and emphasize the Yup'ik value of conserving materials.

6. Distribute the simulated tanned calfskin the students made in Exploration A and ask students to cut the pieces for their small tassels and two center front and back tassels.

7. Demonstrate gluing red yarn on the back at the bottom edge of the two center front and back tassels and the small tassels before they are folded. Also demonstrate adding the white and black yarn for decoration. Fold the paper around your fingers to meet in the back and glue it to form a tube.

8. Distribute red, white, and black yarn to the students and have them complete their small tassels and center front and back tassels.

9. Collect and store the small tassels and the center front and back tassels until the parka is ready for assembly.

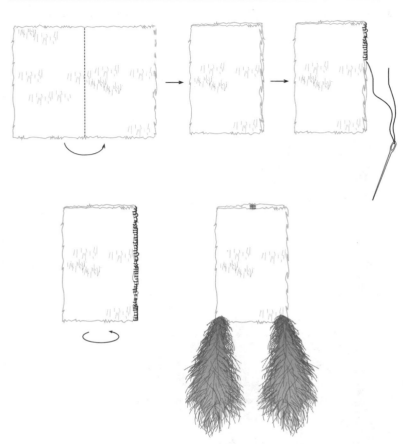

Fig. B.7: Making the small tassels

Assessment

As students work, assess their skill in cutting the irregular pieces of white paper so there is little waste.

Ask students to complete this sentence in their notebooks: "The math I used in making the tassels was . . ."

Annie Blue's Parka, Front

Annie Blue's Parka, Back

Exploration C
Creating a Ruff

The students will create a ruff for a paper parka.

Cultural Note

Yup'ik parkas usually have a ruff layered with two types of fur: long fur such as wolf (*kegluneq*) or wolverine (*terikaniaq*), and short fur such as beaver (*paluqtaq*) or otter (*cuignilnguq*). The traditional ruffs are wide and constructed in layers. The wolf skin is used for the outermost layer and is cut into thin strips and sewn onto thick cloth to form a circle. The strips are sewn with a small space between them, so the ruff appears wide and full. According to Katie George of Akiachak, Alaska, often the strips are sewn onto sealskin. Wolf fur is particularly good for a ruff because ice will not collect on it. The wolverine fur comes next. It is prized for its insulating and protective values. Ice will not collect on it either, which helps protect the wearer's face. The thick, short, soft otter fur is sewn on next to the neck, which helps prevent chafing.

Fig. C.1: Parka ruff Courtesy University of Alaska Museum (#UA68-003-0001)

Goals
- To estimate circumference and work with concentric circles
- To create a ruff for their own parka

Materials
- A large piece of butcher paper for each student
- Actual parka or doll wearing a parka, optional
- Colored pencils
- Markers, three different colors
- Paper ruff for demonstration
- Scissors
- Transparency, Parka Ruff (*Asguruaq*)

Vocabulary

Ruff—oval shaped furs attached to a hood to protect the face and head from the cold.

Oval—the everyday word for the math term ellipse. You can think of an oval as an elongated circle.

Concentric circles—a set of two or more circles that share a common center.

Fig. C.2: Nancy Sharp's classroom in Manokotak, Alaska

Preparation

Make a paper ruff to show the students. Gather and prepare materials and plan to share information with students. See instructions steps 5-7.

Instructions

1. Bring in an actual parka, or a doll wearing a parka, if available.

2. Talk about the many different kinds of materials used by the Yup'ik people to make parkas. Remind students of the severe weather conditions and the need for protection against ice and snow. Show a picture or actual example of the ruff that protects the face and attaches to the hood, optional.

3. Show students a prepared paper ruff or demonstrate making one. Explain that it simulates the fur of the real parka ruff. Show the Parka Ruff to help them visualize the end product.

4. **Discuss.** Ask the students what shape they see for the opening of the ruff. (The general shape of the face is a circle or an oval). This is the shape around which the ruff must fit. Have students estimate their own ruff sizes.

5. **Demonstrate.** Use a body measurement (like one hand span, four finger widths, etc.) to measure the width and length of your face. Transfer the measurement to the center of the butcher paper. Draw an oval that is just a little smaller than your face. (See Figure C.3)

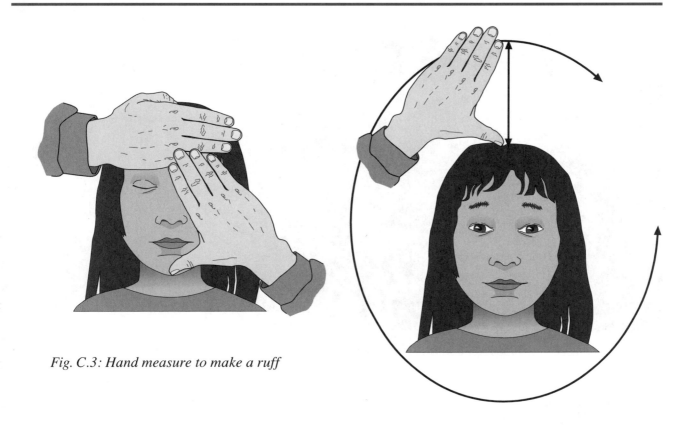

Fig. C.3: Hand measure to make a ruff

6. Use a body measurement of one hand span and draw a larger concentric oval around the first one to designate the limit of the ruff. (See Figure C.3) Use markers to color the three kinds of fur.

7. After the demonstration, have the students create their own ruffs. Have them cut out the larger, outer oval with long fringes. (Refer to Figure C.4) This will simulate the wolf fur.

8. Have them cut out the inner circle so the ruff is ready to paste around the face of the outlined paper parka that students will make in Exploration D.

9. Collect the ruffs when completed and store until it is time for the parka assembly.

Fig. C.4: Boy cutting out a ruff

Parka Ruff (*Asguruaq*)

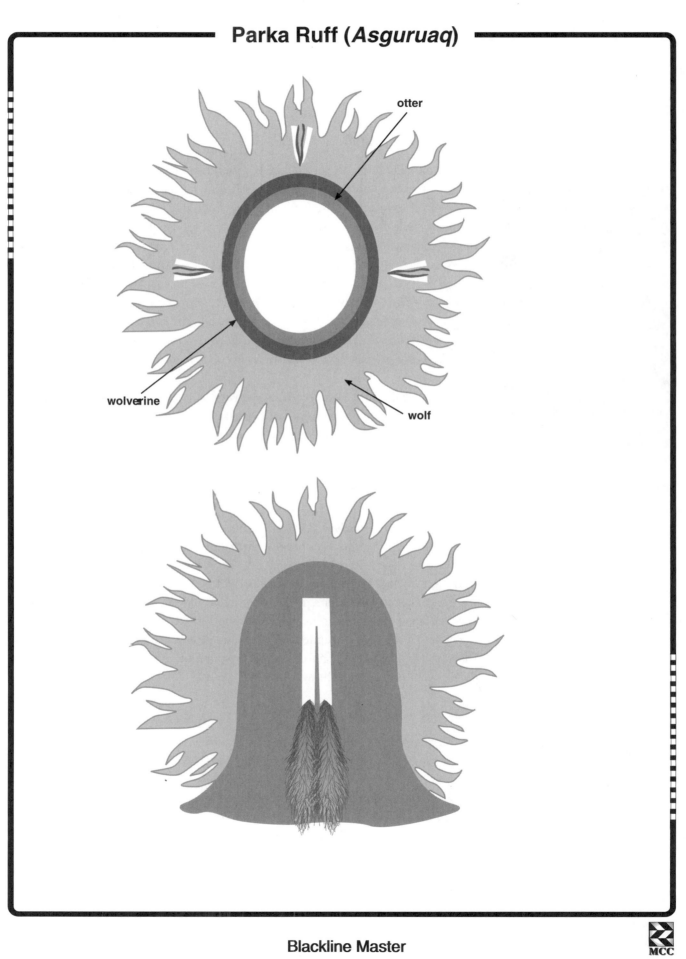

otter

wolverine

wolf

Blackline Master

Exploration D
Creating a Parka

Cultural Note

Yup'ik parkas are frequently made of ground squirrel skin, but they are also made of fox and hoary marmot fur, rabbit skin, caribou hide, and the furs and skins of other animals. More recently, cowhide has been used. Some parkas are even made from bird skins, such as swans, loons, and cormorants. Parkas made from swan skins are worn with the feather side in. The long feathers are removed, leaving only the soft down for insulation. Annie Blue said:

> *People from Asvigyaq [a village] would come to dances and wear parkas made of cormorant skins with rabbit fur ruffs, but the people from Togiak couldn't have that kind because cormorants are ocean birds and my family did not live by the sea [translation].*

Fig. D.1: Student wearing his parka

Other materials were also used to make various types of parkas. Mary Active knew someone who had a parka made of pike fish skins. Raincoats or overcoats were made from walrus or seal gut. Some parkas are made to wear with the fur side in, and often they are made of rabbit fur, which is very soft.

Mary Active commented:

> *I've tried to tan rabbit skins twice, but even while I worked on one it would get very dry and crackly. (Translation)*

Mary Active said her mother would tan a lot of squirrel skins in the fall when the grass was no longer green. "My mother would tan a lot of skins for a long time and then make us parkas." Evelyn Yanez asked: "Did you get a new parka every year?" and Mary replied: "Yes, we got a new parka every year." Annie Blue of Togiak, Alaska, remarked: "Those people were dexterous and they didn't even have good lighting when they sewed."

Mary said:

> *They made parkas and mukluks for us. My mother made all kinds of parkas for me over the years. One time she made me a fox parka and another time of hoary marmots, which are somewhat like raccoons and are excellent for sliding. Yup'ik children loved to go sliding downhill in the snow. A good, strong parka was highly prized because it made sliding easier and more fun.*
>
> *One day my grandmother made a parka for me and came over to have me put it on. I looked at the parka and saw that it was made of*

squirrel skins and didn't have a hood. It just had dark fur trim around the neck and it felt like thin fabric. I wore it for a long time and I even went to sleep in it. It was very comfortable. My mother would try to remove that little parka, but I would fight to keep it on. (Translation)

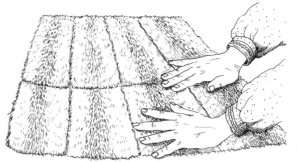

Fig. D.2: Piecing squirrel skins together

The Yup'ik people use the fur of different animals for the decorations. For instance, Annie used coyote or wolf fur for the tassels. Different furs are used for different purposes. Otter fur is short, thick, warm, and very soft. Coyote fur is lighter than wolf. The long guard hairs on coyote, wolf, and wolverine help protect the face from wind and snow. Mary said that one of her sons caught two coyotes in Togiak, another got a white wolf, and her youngest got a dark wolf. Mary skinned the animals, tanned the hides, and used them for sewing decorations on parkas.

Goal
*   To make a paper parka

Materials
*   Actual parka or doll wearing one, optional
*   Colored markers for each student
*   Glue or glue sticks
*   Large pieces of butcher paper for children to draw full-body outlines of each other
*   Parka border designs created in Activity 6 (when completed)
*   Ruff from Exploration C
*   Scissors
*   Tassels from Exploration B

Preparation
Find an appropriate place where students can draw around each other. Gather and prepare materials and plan to share information with students.

Instructions
1. If possible, find someone in your area who makes parkas. Have that person bring in one or more at various stages of completion and explain the process. If an actual parka is not available, a doll wearing a parka can be used.

2. Talk about the many different kinds of materials used by the Yup'ik people to make parkas. Explain that our parkas will be for display, so we will make just the front of a parka. We will decorate it with the tassels and the ruff we created earlier. Also, the border patterns created in Activity 6 may be added when completed.

3. Explain that some Yup'ik parents make new parkas for their children every year. Discuss how students might decide what size to make a parka that fits them. They may think of estimating, using body measurements, using a measuring stick, or lying down on the butcher paper and having someone draw around them.

4. Have students carefully rumple and rub the butcher paper to simulate the effect of tanning. Then have them lay it out flat on the floor, ready for them to outline their partners.

5. Have students work in pairs with one lying down while the other draws around him or her, or use another method of their choosing to make an outline for their parka. Have them sketch their parka over their outlined figure and cut it out.

6. Now that students have outlined and cut out their parkas, they can construct their border patterns by completing Section 1, Activity 6, Part 2 (page 112). They can use their cut out parkas to measure the length needed for their border patterns. When the border pattern is finished they can go on to step 7 and decorate their parkas.

7. Return the envelopes of tassels, the ruffs made earlier, and the border patterns made in Activity 6 when they are completed. Allow time for students to decorate their parkas with the tassels, ruffs, and border patterns.

    Have the students create a display on the bulletin board or other display area with their parkas.

Fig. D.3: Student tracing around another student

Teacher Note

Ideas for Display: Students can draw a face to mount behind the ruff. You may print a picture of each student to mount behind the ruff, or you may have the students cut an opening so they can hold the parka in front of themselves and have their real

Fig. D.4: Squirrel parka with pretend window border

Fig. D.5: An example of a student parka